Emotional Intelligence Simplified

Master Your Emotions, Manage Stress, Enhance
Communication, and Become the Leader Everyone
Respects to Excel in Your Career and Personal Life

Kevin L. Goins

Contents

Introduction

Tom stood up and began to pace back and forth. It was 3:15 pm, and the conference room meeting felt suffocating—not from the heat, but from the heavy fog of unspoken frustrations hanging in the air. The stakes were enormous: a multimillion-dollar project was on the line, and the team was supposed to finalize the launch strategy. Voices clashed, tempers flared, and the tension seemed to cling to every surface like a storm about to erupt. Sarah glanced at her watch, wondering if they'd leave with a solution—or just more reasons to avoid each other in the hallway.

Where was clarity in all of this?

One executive leaned forward, his voice rising as his face flushed crimson. "If we don't act now, we'll lose our edge,' he said, his voice rising just enough to betray the tension he was trying to suppress. He pressed his knuckles against the edge of the table. Across from him, his colleague's eyes narrowed. She leaned back slightly, arms crossed, her words slicing through the silence: 'And if we rush this, we'll lose everything. This isn't just about speed—it's about doing it right.' The room seemed to hold its breath, caught between their opposing worlds.

As voices erupted into shouts, the room descended into chaos.

A junior team member, Julie, eager to contribute, opened her mouth but immediately shrank back as the uproar drowned out her idea. Bob, visibly shaken, sank into his chair, his shoulders rigid and his eyes locked on the clock. Each tick seemed louder than the voices around him. 'I wonder if we'll ever get this done?', he thought. Across the table, a quiet figure raised his hand, his voice steady but soft. 'If we take a moment to—' he began, but his words dissolved into the clamor, unheard.

Everyone wanted to be correct.

Everyone wanted to have their say.

Everyone wanted to talk.

But no one seemed to listen!

Instead of balance and calm, the fight seemed lost, and the meeting's goals remained unmet. Each person left feeling unheard and unseen, wishing that others had listened to them, although they had not been eager to return the favor. The collective lack of emotional control was unmistakable.

The relationships that were once built by having lunch together, dropping by occasionally to exchange ideas, and even going out after work seemed to vanish when it mattered most. If they missed this deadline, what would it cost in missed productivity and ROI for the time spent creating the strategy?

The meeting described above isn't just an isolated event. It's a pattern repeated in boardrooms and offices worldwide. These scenarios and others like them cost productivity, innovation, and morale in the workplace. Left unaddressed, the costs continue to mount.

But what if there were a way to cut through this chaos? To channel the noise into clarity, the tension into collaboration? Emotional intelligence (EI) holds the key. EI is not just a buzzword thrown around corporate settings. Knowing how to become aware of your emotions in heated exchanges and manage them so that you maintain clarity of thought is the secret sauce to having successful outcomes rather than self-destructive ones.

EI doesn't involve suppressing emotions—it requires understanding them. It's the ability to recognize when emotions are running the show and to steer them back toward meaningful progress.

The purpose of this book is to serve as a transformative guide for ambitious professionals like you to become aware of a hidden power that exists within by knowing what to do when emotions arise in various setting. Whether you're a corporate worker, a manager, or a leader, mastering EI can be a game-changer in your career and personal life. This book is your guide to harnessing that power—to calm the storms, sharpen focus, and create lasting impact in every room you step into. You will find actionable strategies and insights designed to help you navigate the complexities of your professional environment while maintaining personal balance.

My target audience consists of adults who are driven by professional development and personal growth. You are the problem solvers, innovators, and those who seek a harmonious balance between work and life. This book will aid your journey to becoming the leader everyone respects.

My unique perspective is how using language and observations versus judgments can enhance EI working on your behalf. This idea shifts the view of EI from an inherent trait to a skill that can be developed. By changing the way we speak to ourselves and others, especially during stressful situations, we can pause, reflect, and choose a response that aligns with our goals rather than react viscerally in the moment.

My vision is to encourage investment in emotional education programs. EI is not just a nice-to-have; it is vital for effective leadership and personal well-being. Through this book, I hope to inspire you to see EI as a critical component of your personal and professional toolkit.

The book is structured around key themes that will resonate with you. We will explore how to differentiate between who you are as a person versus how well you perform a task, how to shift from judgment to observation, and how to use empowering language to your advantage. Additionally, we will deep-dive into stress management techniques so that if your body reacts to scenarios throughout your workday, you have the tools to choose to redirect and respond instead.

With you in mind, I put this book together so you can easily find actionable strategies, exercises, examples, and case studies without reading it from beginning to end. It is designed to be practical, enabling you to read it from cover to cover or skip straight to the section you need to address a real-life scenario using the principles immediately. Whether handling a difficult conversation or managing stress, you will have the tools you need to succeed while having a more in-depth understanding of your emotional response.

This book seeks to shine a light on understanding emotional intelligence, as well as changing how you experience it daily. Imagine having the tools to navigate challenging conversations. Is it possible you may not always get it right every single time even with the tools? Absolutely. That's part of our human growth journey of being exposed to a new concept and then learning to embrace and practice it. Using the tools repeatedly allows you to release the feeling of overwhelm and enhances your ability to connect deeply with your team while staying true to your values. These skills are life-changing abilities that can shape your career and relationships in ways you never thought possible.

I'm not here to give you generic advice. I'm here to offer practical strategies and real-life examples that you can apply immediately so that the next time a high-stakes meeting occurs, you can be that voice of reason that is not afraid to speak up, emotionally intelligently, with clarity.

I invite you to disrupt old ways of reacting by adopting new strategies and ways of thinking so that you get different results. In the process, you will uncover disempowering thought patterns that may be holding you back. You have the opportunity to redefine what success could look like—personally and professionally.

Let's embark on this journey together. By the end of this book, you will understand and live with emotional intelligence.

1. Understanding Emotional Intelligence

I magine: Jessica froze mid-sentence during the presentation, and the room fell silent. She had been preparing for this moment for months, putting in countless hours, team meetings, and work-from-home input. Yet, when it was time for her to present, her lips parted as if to speak, but nothing came out. "I know this", she thought. But the result? Silence.

Her knuckles turned white as she gripped the podium tighter, and her eyes darted briefly to the door as if she were ready to sprint out of it. The audience shifted uncomfortably, unsure whether to step in to help her or let her find her way. The presentation, and perhaps the client's confidence, teetered on the edge of collapse.

Moments like this happen more often than we admit and test more than just our preparation—they test how we respond to our emotions and manage them when they arise. In high-pressure environments, where deadlines loom, and relationships are critical, knowing how to navigate these situations with empathy and poise separates a thriving team from a fractured one.

1.1 Emotional Intelligence Demystified

Emotional intelligence (EI) is the ability to understand, manage, and express emotions in a way that works for you and strengthens your relationships with others. It involves more than just "feeling" emotions—it's about recognizing them, staying in control, and responding to life's challenges with clarity and compassion. It also encourages you to connect with people, understand their feelings, and approach interactions with care and good judgment. Daniel Goleman, a leading voice in emotional intelligence, breaks it down into four key areas: self-awareness, self-regulation, social awareness, and relationship management.

Let's start with self-awareness, the cornerstone of EI. It involves tuning into your emotions, recognizing their impact, and understanding how they shape your actions. For example, when you're frustrated during a tense moment, self-awareness helps you notice that frustration before it influences your behavior. It's like turning on a light in a room you've walked through in the dark—you suddenly see what's there, and it all starts to make sense.

Then comes self-regulation, which builds on self-awareness. It teaches you to manage those emotions, stay calm under pressure, and respond thoughtfully instead of reacting impulsively. Imagine being able to pause, take a breath, and choose how to respond when a colleague criticizes your work or when life throws an unexpected curveball. That's the power of self-regulation—it creates space for clarity and level-headed decisions when needed most.

Next is social awareness, which shifts the focus outward. It's the ability to pick up on the emotions of others—to see beyond their words and into their feelings. This skill helps you read the room, sense when someone is upset, or recognize when somebody may need encouragement. It is grounded in empathy: understanding someone else's perspective and showing you care.

Finally, relationship management ties everything together. When you combine self-awareness, self-regulation, and social awareness, you gain the ability to build meaningful connections, resolve conflicts, and inspire cooperation. It's what allows a leader to rally a team or helps a parent navigate hard conversations with her teenager.

Despite its importance, EI is often misunderstood. Some people think emotional intelligence is something you're either born with or not, but that's far from the truth. Like any skill, EI can be developed with time and effort. It doesn't require us to always be agreeable or avoid tough conversations. Instead, it encourages us to set boundaries, make hard decisions, and communicate honestly, even when our emotions run high.

Another misconception is that EI is just about expressing feelings, but that's only part of the picture. Emotional intelligence focuses on understanding and managing emotions—not letting them take over. This book aims to cut through these myths and show you how to develop EI as a practical skill that can benefit anyone willing to put in the work.

The impact of emotional intelligence goes well beyond work. In leadership roles, EI creates a culture where employees feel valued and understood, boosting morale and productivity. It's the glue that holds teams together, especially during conflicts, helping to foster collaboration rather than division. At home, EI can also strengthen relationships, helping you handle disagreements more effectively and creating a sense of harmony. It's also a powerful tool for managing stress, equipping you to handle life's pressures with grace and resilience. Whether it's resolving family arguments, building trust at work, or simply maintaining mental well-being, EI is at the heart of personal and professional success.

Think of emotional intelligence as a kind of fitness for your mind and relationships. Just like lifting weights strengthens your body, practicing EI reinforces your ability to navigate emotions and connect with others. Exercises like mindfulness help you become more self-aware while empathy-building activities enhance your understanding of others. These skills aren't abstract; they're tools you can develop and use every day.

As a speaker, facilitator, and executive coach, I've seen firsthand how EI is improved in countless people through structured workshops and coaching, both in person and virtually. By investing in this kind of growth, you're not just improving your career, you're enriching your personal relationships and paving the way for a more balanced, fulfilling life. I believe that this is a journey worth taking, and the benefits will ripple through practically every aspect of your world.

1.2 The Science Behind Emotional Intelligence

The way emotions influence decision-making reveals just how intricate and dynamic the human mind truly is. At the heart of this process is the limbic system, a network of brain structures responsible for regulating emotional responses. Often called the "emotional brain," the limbic system interacts with the prefrontal cortex, or the "rational brain," to shape our perceptions and choices. When emotions run high, the limbic system can take over, leading to decisions driven more by instinct than careful thought. Recognizing when emotions are at play helps us take a step back, reflect, and make decisions that align with our values and goals. This practice is key to emotional intelligence, allowing us to avoid impulsive choices that might create unnecessary challenges in both personal and professional settings.

Emotional intelligence is rooted in biological processes that govern how we respond to the world. A central player in this process is the amygdala, an almond-shaped structure within the limbic system. The amygdala acts as the brain's emotional alarm system, processing emotions like fear, anger, and pleasure. In moments of stress or perceived threat, the amygdala can override rational thinking, prompting quick, instinctive reactions. Meanwhile, the prefrontal cortex—located at the front of the brain—helps regulate these emotions. It allows us to evaluate situations, plan our responses, and maintain control over impulsive actions. The balance between the amygdala and prefrontal cortex is essential for emotional regulation, which is a core element of emotional intelligence. Research shows that individuals with higher EI tend to have stronger connections between these regions, enhancing their ability to manage emotions and make thoughtful decisions.

Numerous studies highlight the advantages of emotional intelligence across different areas of life. For example:

- **In Leadership:** Leaders with high emotional intelligence tend to excel at managing teams, resolving conflicts, and cultivating a positive workplace culture. Research supports that emotionally intelligent leaders are more effective in motivating others and achieving organizational goals.
- **In Career Growth:** High EI is often linked to professional success. People with strong EI skills tend to rise quickly in their careers, navigate workplace dynamics with ease, and build more robust networks. Their ability to remain approachable and composed makes them stand out to colleagues and leaders alike.

Unchecked emotions can easily skew decision-making. Biases like overconfidence, fear, or emotional attachment often lead to poor choices. In the workplace, this might look like a manager making snap decisions out of fear or a team member staying silent due to anxiety. Recognizing these emotional influences is the first step toward counteracting them. By identifying and addressing biases, we can create strategies that promote balanced, objective decisions. Case studies consistently show that emotional regulation leads to clearer thinking, more collaborative environments, and better outcomes overall.

Ever wonder why some appear more calm at work than others, even when it is a high-pressure job? The benefits of emotional intelligence extend far beyond professional success. One of its most immediate advantages is stress reduction, which creates a sense of calm. With greater emotional awareness, individuals can identify stressors and address them proactively. For some, this is natural, and they navigate this without thinking. However, with practice, this skill can also be developed.

When paired with emotional regulation skills, this awareness builds resilience, helping people face challenges with calm and confidence. Beyond managing stress, EI fosters a sense of inner stability, promoting mental and emotional well-being. It equips individuals to handle life's ups and downs with grace, making it a powerful tool for cultivating holistic growth and balance.

By understanding the role emotions play in decision-making, relationships, and personal growth, emotional intelligence becomes a practical and transformative skill that creates surprising results.

1.3 Emotional Intelligence vs. IQ vs. EQ: Clarifying the Key Differences

When it comes to understanding success—both personal and professional—three terms often come up: **intelligence quotient (IQ)**, **emotional intelligence (EI)**, **and emotional quotient (EQ)**. While interconnected, each serves a distinct purpose, and understanding these differences can help you unlock your full potential.

IQ, or intelligence quotient, measures cognitive abilities such as logical reasoning, problem-solving, and analytical thinking. It's a gauge of intellectual capacity, often assessed through standardized tests that predict academic potential or technical skill. Think of IQ as the foundation of "what you know" and how well you can solve complex, analytical problems.

On the other hand, EQ, or emotional quotient, measures emotional intelligence. While IQ evaluates how well you think, EQ measures how well you understand and manage emotions—both your own and those of others. It focuses on human connection, including reading social cues, empathizing, resolving conflicts, and leading with emotional insight.

Here's an example to illustrate: A high-IQ individual might design the perfect project plan, but a high-EQ leader ensures the team feels valued and motivated to execute that plan. While IQ focuses on technical precision, EQ is the driving force of building trust, loyalty, and collaboration.

Throughout this book, I primarily refer to emotional intelligence (EI) instead of EQ. Why? Because emotional intelligence isn't just something to measure—it's a skill to develop, practice, and apply in everyday life. For simplicity, I'll use EI as the core term to help you focus on what emotional intelligence means and how to leverage it, rather than just how to measure it. While the term EQ might appear on the cover, this book is designed to cut through the jargon and give you practical tools to build your EI.

Let's explore how IQ and EI complement each other. Imagine a leader with a high IQ but limited emotional intelligence. They might excel at strategic planning but struggle to connect with their team, leading to disengagement or conflict. Now, picture someone with a modest IQ but exceptional EI. Their ability to empathize, communicate, and build relationships often outweighs technical expertise in roles that require leadership or teamwork.

As we dive deeper, you'll see why emotional intelligence (EI) matters so much in today's world. While IQ gives you the tools to think critically, EI ensures you can apply those tools in a way that inspires connection, trust, and collaboration. Whether you're navigating personal relationships, leading a team, or managing stress, EI is what transforms knowledge into meaningful action.

1.4 The Transformative Power of Emotional Intelligence in Leadership

The ability to guide and inspire others relies heavily on emotional intelligence. A leader's capacity to motivate teams depends on their skill in forming genuine emotional connections with those they serve. Imagine a manager who not only understands the technical aspects of a project but also the emotional undercurrents that drive their team. This leader recognizes the subtle signs of stress in a team member's voice and offers support before it becomes overwhelming. Here, trust is cultivated through emotional understanding. When team members feel seen and heard, they are more likely to trust their leader and feel motivated to contribute their best efforts. Emotional intelligence fosters an environment where empathy and support are paramount, allowing for a team dynamic that thrives on collaboration and mutual respect.

Leadership styles vary, but those that successfully integrate emotional intelligence often stand out for their effectiveness. Transformational leadership, for example, emphasizes inspiring and motivating followers to achieve more than they thought possible. This style leverages emotional intelligence by creating a vision that resonates on a personal level, encouraging team members to invest emotionally in their work. Similarly, servant leadership revolves around prioritizing the needs of others, fostering an atmosphere where empathy and emotional understanding are integral. Such leaders engage with their teams on a deeply emotional level, ensuring that each member feels valued and supported.

Emotional transparency is a powerful tool in building authentic relationships within a team. Leaders who practice emotional regulation while maintaining transparency create a space where honesty is appreciated. By sharing emotions within appropriate boundaries, they demonstrate vulnerability, which can strengthen trust. Expressing genuine feelings without oversharing allows leaders to connect with their teams, showing that they, too, experience challenges. This openness fosters a sense of belonging, encouraging team members to express their thoughts and feelings without fear of judgment.

Several leaders have set benchmarks in emotional intelligence. Nelson Mandela's empathetic approach during his presidency exemplifies how understanding and compassion can unite a nation divided by years of apartheid. His ability to listen and empathize with both allies and adversaries alike helped to foster reconciliation. In a more contemporary context, New Zealand's Prime Minister Jacinda Ardern has demonstrated exceptional emotional intelligence in crisis management, particularly during the Christchurch mosque shootings. Her empathetic response and authentic communication provided solace to a grieving nation, showcasing how emotional intelligence in leadership can guide entire communities through adversity.

Practical strategies are crucial for those who aspire to develop their emotional intelligence in leadership. Role-playing exercises can enhance empathy by allowing leaders to experience different perspectives. These exercises promote understanding and improve communication skills. Emotional feedback loops, where leaders seek and reflect on feedback from their teams, can drive self-improvement. This continuous cycle of feedback and reflection helps leaders fine-tune their emotional responses, fostering an environment of growth and mutual respect.

As we conclude this exploration of emotional intelligence in leadership, consider the lasting impact that emotionally intelligent leaders can have. They inspire trust, motivate teams, and create authentic connections that redefine success. By cultivating these skills, leaders enhance their effectiveness and transform the environments in which they operate. Emotional intelligence is the key to unlocking a leader's true potential, paving the way for a more connected and compassionate future.

2. Overcoming Barriers to Emotional Intelligence

Picture a skilled manager, widely respected for their technical brilliance, stepping into a pivotal team meeting with high expectations. But instead of steering the discussion effectively, they find themselves stumbling. The room feels tense, conversations falter, and their well-prepared ideas don't land as they imagined. They're so focused on the agenda that they miss the subtle cues—the furrowed brows, the uneasy body language, the silence that speaks volumes. By the end of the meeting, the disconnect is palpable, leaving the manager frustrated and their team disengaged. Their career, once full of momentum, feels at risk of stalling—not because of a lack of expertise, but because of an inability to connect.

While this scenario is fictional, it's all too familiar for many professionals. They excel in the technical skills that earned them their roles but struggle to navigate the emotional landscapes of team dynamics, leadership, and collaboration. What they lack isn't intelligence nor talent—it's emotional intelligence (EI), the often-overlooked key to unlocking personal and professional potential. Without it, even the brightest minds can hit a ceiling, unable to lead effectively, build trust, or inspire those around them.

One of the biggest hurdles is the misunderstanding of what emotional intelligence truly is. Some think it's about being overly emotional or letting feelings run the show, while others dismiss it as a soft skill that doesn't carry weight in high-stakes environments. These misconceptions create barriers, preventing professionals from tapping into their full potential. EI doesn't mean suppressing emotions or being overly accommodating—it encourages you to understand and manage your emotions, while recognizing and responding to the emotions of others. It's the bridge between technical expertise and the ability to lead, influence, and create meaningful connections.

Think about it: How many brilliant ideas go unheard because the presenter can't read their audience? How many projects derail because leaders miss the underlying concerns of their teams? Without EI, opportunities for growth, collaboration, and innovation slip through the cracks. But with it, those same professionals can transform challenges into opportunities, creating an environment where people feel understood, valued, and inspired to give their best.

If this resonates with you, consider this: EI isn't an innate trait reserved for the lucky few—it's a skill that can be developed. And for those willing to invest in it, the rewards are significant. From stronger relationships to career breakthroughs, emotional intelligence has the power to take you further than technical skills alone ever could. What would change for you if you started cultivating it today?

2.1 Overcoming Resistance to Emotional Growth

One of the most persistent myths about emotional intelligence is that it's an innate gift—you either have it or you don't. This idea is as misleading as it is discouraging. Viewing EI as fixed can cause resistance to growth, as people feel powerless to change. However, emotional intelligence is not static; it's a skill that can be developed with intention and effort, like learning a language or mastering a sport.

I've often seen this resistance in the workplace. I remember working in a professional setting years back where technology was high, but the user's understanding of how to use that technology to get the job done was at an all-time low. No matter how often we called for support to help, they would take their time answering and even scoff at those who didn't know which buttons to push to get the desired result. You almost felt unintelligent asking for help. Those promoted tended to know the most about the technology. Still, their people skills and ability to lead were noticeably lacking. Emotional intelligence would have enhanced connections with the users and collaboration in team settings.

To overcome resistance to emotional intelligence, start with small steps. Instead of framing EI development as a daunting overhaul, approach it as incremental progress. Begin by observing your emotions. Notice how you feel in different situations. Try not to judge yourself. Just notice. Practice empathy during everyday interactions. For example, actively listen when someone shares their thoughts, ask open-ended questions, and acknowledge their feelings without offering solutions. The key is to focus on progress from consistent effort that builds momentum over time.

Reflection Questions

- Do you believe emotional intelligence is something you can grow? Why or why not?
- What's one small way you could begin improving your EI today?
- How do you typically react to emotionally charged situations, and what might you do differently?

2.2 Learning from Failures: Emotional Intelligence in Setbacks

Failure often triggers emotions like frustration, disappointment, or even shame. Yet, as challenging as these moments may feel, they are fertile ground for developing emotional intelligence. When viewed through the right lens, setbacks become opportunities to practice self-awareness, self-regulation, and empathy—skills that form the foundation of EI.

For example, consider a colleague whose anxiety about public speaking once led to a disastrous presentation in front of senior leadership. Overwhelmed with embarrassment and self-doubt, they initially wanted to avoid similar situations altogether. However, instead of retreating, they chose to confront their fears head-on. They began by seeking honest feedback from trusted peers, which helped them pinpoint areas for improvement. They enrolled in a public speaking workshop, practiced regularly in intimate group settings, and adopted techniques such as visualization and controlled breathing to manage their nerves. Through persistence and practice, they strengthened their technical presentation skills and gained confidence in their ability to connect with an audience. Over time, this transformation earned them recognition as one of their organization's most effective and engaging speakers, illustrating how failures can serve as powerful catalysts for growth.

What society calls failure, which often has a negative stigma attached, is where we learn our greatest lessons. Failures teach us what we need to improve and how to better understand ourselves and others in various settings, especially those that may appear difficult or overwhelming. Acknowledging our emotional responses and owning how we navigate setbacks can turn obstacles into stepping stones.

Reflection Questions

- Think of a recent setback. How did your emotions shape your response?
- How might viewing failure as a learning opportunity shift your perspective?
- What emotional skills could help you better navigate future challenges?

2.3 Addressing Skepticism and Misconceptions

A common misconception is that emotional intelligence (EI) is less important than IQ in achieving success. EI can be dismissed as "soft" or irrelevant in highly technical fields. But research—and real-world experience—tells a different story. For example, FedEx implemented a leadership development program centered on EI. Over six months, managers were coached on aligning their behaviors with professional goals and transitioning from reactive habits to intentional responses. The results were undeniable: improved decision-making, better relationships, and measurable gains in leadership effectiveness.

Similarly, emotional intelligence is sometimes confined to personal interactions, seen as being more useful at home than in the boardroom. But consider this: how often do professional successes hinge on interpersonal dynamics? From securing a promotion to leading a team through change, the ability to connect and empathize is invaluable. Emotional intelligence is not a "soft skill"; it's a strategic one.

Skepticism can also stem from discomfort. It's easier to hide behind technical expertise than to embrace vulnerability. A client I once coached excelled in data analysis but struggled to lead her team. She admitted, "I just don't want to look weak by talking about emotions." She tended to suppress her emotions and only focused on her accomplishments, leaving her to feel the connection to her team was missing. Over time, as she practiced empathetic listening and acknowledged her emotional responses, she found that her team's engagement and trust skyrocketed.

Addressing these misconceptions requires education, real-life examples, and open dialogue. By understanding that EI complements IQ and technical skills, professionals can unlock their full potential and foster more meaningful connections.

Reflection Questions

- Have you ever dismissed emotional intelligence as less important than technical skills? If so, why?
- What's one way you've seen EI (or the lack of it) impact workplace dynamics?
- How might embracing emotional intelligence enhance your personal or professional life?

Challenging the barriers to emotional intelligence begins with a willingness to question assumptions. Instead of attempting to overhaul who you are, practice taking intentional steps toward growth. By addressing resistance, learning from failures, and debunking misconceptions, you can cultivate emotional intelligence as a practical, transformative tool.

Reflection Questions

- What myths about emotional intelligence have you believed?
- How might those beliefs have influenced your approach to relationships and success?
- What's one action you can take today to begin breaking down barriers to your own emotional growth?

Through education, practice, and reflection, emotional intelligence becomes a skill that enhances every aspect of life. Whether you're leading a team, navigating a personal setback, or simply striving to connect more deeply with others, EI offers a path to greater awareness, resilience, and fulfillment.

3. Self-Awareness: The Foundation of Emotional Intelligence

You are in a busy office, juggling an unexpected crisis on a Monday morning. The phone won't stop ringing, emails are piling up, and your team turns to you for guidance. Underneath the external disarray of things, an internal storm is brewing—a spark of irritation from an abrupt email, a tight feeling in your chest from an offhand remark. These emotional reactions aren't random; they're your emotional triggers at work, shaped by life experiences and quietly influencing your thoughts and actions.

Your emotional triggers are those situations or interactions that ignite strong reactions, often out of proportion to the moment. They're rooted in deeply ingrained memories and experiences, especially from childhood. These early life events shape how we perceive trust, safety, and self-worth, laying the foundation for our emotional responses as adults. For example, if you grew up around constant criticism, you might be extra sensitive to feedback. On the other hand, a supportive environment might help you handle challenges with resilience. As you move through life, social interactions further shape these triggers. A slight from a coworker or a disagreement with a friend can leave a mark, influencing how you handle similar situations down the road.

In the workplace, specific scenarios that you encounter may provoke strong emotions. Remember your tight deadline that triggered anxiety as the date loomed closer? How did that feel as the pressure mounted? A sharp email from your boss could spark feelings of inadequacy or anger. These stressors are familiar to many of us. Similarly, personal challenges like family disputes or financial strain can awaken old emotional patterns, spilling into professional settings.

If left unacknowledged, these reactions can escalate, leading to outbursts or clouded decision-making. In high-stakes environments, unchecked emotions can ripple through a team, destabilizing morale and undermining trust in leadership.

When these emotional triggers go unnoticed, they can result in impulsive reactions or prolonged stress. In decision-making, they steer you toward knee-jerk responses to satisfy the moment instead of thoughtful ones that may take time and effort. Visualize a manager whose fear of failure, rooted in childhood memories of disappointing his parents with anything less than straight A's, causes him to make a rash decision that impacts the entire team. Or think of a colleague whose emotional responses disrupt team harmony, creating misunderstandings and tension. Emotional triggers inform your pending actions and decisions so that you make the ones you prefer. The goal is to use the information that the triggers carry constructively. However, the triggers tend to take over, making the situation a bigger deal than it is if left unchecked.

Identifying these triggers takes effort and self-reflection. Journaling is a helpful tool that allows you to track your emotional responses over time. You can begin spotting patterns and understanding what sets off strong reactions by writing down your own thoughts. A "trigger diary" can provide valuable insight into interactions or contexts that evoke intense emotions. Reflecting on challenging days or heated moments is another strategy. After a stressful event, ask yourself: What caused this reaction? Do specific themes keep repeating? These exercises can help you trace your emotional responses back to their roots.

Take the story of a professional athlete who struggled with anxiety before significant games. By realizing that his anxiety stemmed from childhood pressures to perform, he began working with a coach to address these emotional triggers. Through journaling and self-reflection, he turned his anxiety into focused energy. Similarly, a manager who reacted defensively to feedback discovered her sensitivity came from a history of harsh criticism. By recognizing this pattern, she learned to view feedback as an opportunity to grow, not a personal attack. These examples show the power of understanding emotional triggers—they transform obstacles into opportunities for growth and connection.

Reflection Time

What areas of your life do memories trigger emotional reactions emotionally when similar situations arise?

3.1 Judgment vs. Observation: Shifting Perspectives

In the fast pace of daily life, it's easy to fall into judgmental thinking. Maybe you glance at a colleague's cluttered desk and think, "They're so messy." Or when a team member misses a deadline, you jump to the conclusion that they're unreliable. These snap judgments often lead to frustration or irritation and shape how we see others. But they're based on assumptions, not facts. And it's not your fault!

Your brain is like a master efficiency expert. Once it figures out how to do something, it's wired to stick with what works. That's why repeating a task feels effortless—it's your brain leaning on a familiar process rather than starting from scratch. Over time, these repeated actions strengthen specific neural pathways, turning them into shortcuts that save energy. In neuroscience, this process of the brain is referred to as generalizing. You see this daily in habits like typing on a keyboard or making coffee. What once took effort becomes second nature, running on autopilot so you can focus on new things. With daily tasks, it is useful not to think of each step. Autopilot is essential for generalizing tasks because you no longer have to think! On the other hand, with humans, generalizing is usually *not* a good thing.

When we encounter a situation involving people, our brain, just as it would do concerning tasks, instinctively tries to conserve energy by quickly assigning the situation meaning based on what it already knows. The brain assumes it understands the situation and whether that assumption is accurate. Generalizing with people is a process we often call judgment. The problem with judgment is that it relies heavily on experiences and assumptions, which can block us from seeing or learning something new about the other person. Mindlessly assigning meaning to people is where leaders may want to improve. At this step of the brain's process, we might blunder and create disconnection with judgment rather than connection through observation.

For example, a specific event or detail might explain what's happening, but if our brain skips over that and fills in the gaps with assumptions, we can miss the real story. Assumptions exclude important pieces of context, which can make others feel ignored or misunderstood. And let's be honest—when people feel unheard or dismissed, it's easy for frustration and resentment to take root. It's a reminder that listening and seeking understanding helps us connect and grow. Pausing to observe in order to avoid judging may feel awkward to do at first, but with time and practice, as with any skill, it will feel more normal.

Observational thinking offers a healthier alternative because it stops the generalizing/judgment process before the judgment is fully underway. Instead of thinking, "They're disorganized," you might note, "Their desk is cluttered." This perspective removes the emotional charge and opens the door to curiosity. Instead of judging someone, you might wonder, "What's been keeping them so busy?" There may be things that you do not know unless you ask.

This shift from judgment to observation greatly impacts your emotional well-being. Judgmental thinking fuels tension and stress that you create for yourself and others, while observational thinking fosters neutrality and understanding. Notice that in both situations, whether you judge or choose to observe, the fact is that the choice lies with you. The process occurs in your brain. No one else is there, so you are responsible for creating your peace and calm each day by how you choose to think.

Observation calms the mind, encourages empathy, and creates space for collaboration. Observational thinking can transform conflicts into opportunities for dialogue. When you pause to ask questions instead of jumping to conclusions, you create an environment of openness and trust.

Practicing observational thinking requires focus and patience. Techniques like meditation can help. By focusing on the present moment, you train yourself to notice your thoughts and feelings without attaching judgments. Reframing exercises are also helpful. To reframe, when you notice yourself making a judgment—such as "They're so lazy" or "I can't believe they didn't think this through"—pause and follow these steps:

A Step-by-Step Guide to Reframing Judgments into Observations

1. **Pause and Acknowledge the Judgment**
   - Recognize the thought for what it is: a judgment, not a fact. Acknowledge it without self-criticism.
     - Example: "I just judged my coworker as lazy for missing a deadline."
2. **Separate Facts from Assumptions**
   - Ask yourself: What do I know for certain, and what am I assuming?

- - Fact: "The deadline was missed."
  - Assumption: "They didn't care enough to complete the task."

3. **Reframe with Neutral Language**
   - Turn the judgment into a neutral observation by describing what happened without attaching a value.
     - Observation: "The deadline was missed, and I'm unsure why."

4. **Consider Alternative Explanations**
   - Practice empathy by imagining other reasons for the situation.
     - Thought: "Maybe they were overwhelmed or misunderstood the timeline."

5. **Take a Constructive Next Step**
   - Use your observation to decide on a constructive action, such as asking questions for clarification or offering support.
     - Action: "I'll check in to understand what happened and how we can avoid this in the future."

In action, observational thinking can transform interactions. Think about a tense meeting where opinions clash. A judgmental mindset might cause defensiveness and escalate the conflict. However, if everyone adopts an observational approach, they can focus on the facts and work toward solutions. Similarly, in personal relationships, observing instead of judging can ease tension. Instead of criticizing a partner for being late, you could say, "I noticed you arrived later than planned," and open a conversation about what happened.

Recognizing that you hold the power to create your peace of mind—or disrupt it—by choosing to observe rather than judge can be a pivotal realization. Judgment often becomes our default simply because we don't fully understand how the brain operates in its natural, untrained state. Shifting your energy inward and focusing on your responses, rather than projecting outward, can dramatically accelerate your personal growth and emotional awareness. As a result, your ability to connect with others, build influence, and foster genuine relationships will naturally expand.

3.2 Tools for Self-Assessment and Personal Insight

Building emotional intelligence is like developing any other skill; it requires regular practice and honest evaluation. Self-assessment tools are a great place to start. These evaluation tools measure an individual's emotional intelligence in the areas of self-awareness, self-regulation, social awareness, and relationship management, clearly showing where one is strong and where one could improve.

Feedback from peers and mentors is also invaluable. While self-assessments give you an internal perspective, others can offer insights you might miss. Colleagues can highlight how your emotions appear in team settings, and mentors can guide you through challenges. Combining self-assessment with external feedback gives you a fuller picture of your emotional skills.

Consistency is key to getting the most out of these tools. Regular check-ins help you track your progress and stay accountable. Approach assessments with honesty and openness, even when it's uncomfortable. By facing areas of weakness, you set the stage for growth. Over time, revisiting these assessments can show how far you've come and keep you on track.

3.3 A Practical Guide on How to Conduct Regular Check-ins

Regular check-ins serve as critical milestones on the journey of emotional development, offering a structured framework for monitoring advancements, engaging in sincere self-reflection, and fine-tuning your emotional strategies accordingly. Embracing these structured check-ins illuminates the intricate patterns of your emotional behaviors, providing a clear path to addressing them and fostering sustained emotional intelligence growth. To optimize the benefits derived from these reflective sessions, adhere to the following detailed guide:

1. **Schedule Consistent Times for Reflection**
   - Choose specific times in your day or week to pause and evaluate your emotional state. Consistency helps establish this practice as a natural part of your daily life.
     - **Daily:** Spend 5–10 minutes in the morning, midday, and evening.
     - **Weekly:** Dedicate 15–30 minutes at the end of the week for a more in-depth review, allowing for broader insights and adjustments.
2. **Create a Safe Space for Reflection**
   - Find a quiet, distraction-free environment where you can focus on your inner self without interruptions. This might be a corner of your home, a quiet park, or even your car before starting work.
3. **Ask Specific, Guiding Questions**
   - The key to effective check-ins is asking meaningful questions that encourage honest reflection. Consider these prompts:
     - **Morning Check-In:**
       - What emotional state do I want to cultivate today?
       - What is one small action I can take to stay grounded and focused?
     - **Midday Check-In:**
       - How am I feeling right now, and what triggered this emotion?
       - Have I acted in alignment with my emotional goals for the day?
       - What adjustments can I make to improve the rest of my day?
     - **Evening Check-In:**
       - What were the highlights of my day, and how did they make me feel?

- What challenges did I face, and how did I handle them emotionally?
- What would I like to carry forward into tomorrow?

4. **Use Tracking Tools to Log Insights**
   - Write down your reflections to track progress over time. Use tools that work best for you:
     - **Journals:** Write entries by hand or digitally to capture your thoughts and patterns.
     - **Spreadsheets:** Create columns for the date, emotions, triggers, actions, and lessons learned.
     - **Phone Notes:** Keep quick, on-the-go observations in your phone's notes app.

5. **Celebrate Small Wins and Identify Patterns**
   - **Celebrate Wins:** Note moments when you handled a situation with greater emotional awareness or effectively managed stress. Recognizing progress boosts motivation.
   - **Identify Patterns:** Look for recurring triggers, emotional responses, or behaviors. These patterns provide valuable insights into areas for growth.

6. **Be Honest and Gentle with Yourself**
   - Regular check-ins are not meant for self-criticism—they're opportunities for awareness and growth. When reflecting on areas for improvement, frame them constructively:
     - Instead of: "I'm terrible at staying calm during meetings."
     - Try: "I noticed that I struggled to stay calm today. Next time, I'll try taking a few deep breaths before responding."

7. **Revisit and Adjust Your Goals**
   - Use insights from your check-ins to refine your emotional goals. As you grow, you might set more specific intentions or explore new areas of emotional intelligence to develop.

The real value of self-assessments lies in the deeper analysis of the results. Look for patterns in your emotional responses. Are there recurring situations where you struggle? Do you notice themes in how you interact with others? These patterns can reveal the roots of your emotional habits, giving you the insight needed to address them.

Consider the case of a corporate leader who used 360-degree feedback to improve her emotional intelligence. By gathering input from colleagues, superiors, and subordinates, she saw how her defensive reactions in meetings affected team dynamics. With this awareness, she worked on regulating her emotions, leading to better collaboration and trust. Similarly, a student preparing for a career in human resources used emotional intelligence assessments to refine her skills. She discovered strengths like empathy and listening but also identified areas like assertiveness that needed work. These tools helped her focus on personal growth and career success.

Understanding and managing emotions is the linchpin of emotional intelligence. By identifying triggers, shifting perspectives, and using self-assessment tools, you can build a strong foundation for growth. Next, we'll explore how self-management builds on this foundation, empowering you to use emotional intelligence in robust, practical ways.

4. Self-Management: Mastering Your Emotions

4.1 Emotional Patterns: What Are They & Why Do They Matter?

Have you ever overreacted to feedback, misinterpreting someone's honesty and attempts to improve the process as harsh criticism? Perhaps you felt irritated to the point of defensiveness. Then, somehow, you took it personally and became angry, releasing your emotions and trying to find a way to apologize for your overreaction. When someone provides feedback and touches your triggers, is your default response to feel defensive or reactive? Beneath these immediate reactions lies a deeper pattern—an ingrained response to criticism that has developed over the years. These emotional patterns, often operating under the radar, have a powerful impact on how we behave and make decisions.

Emotional patterns are like the automatic scripts we follow when life throws us into situations involving criticism, praise, or conflict. Often shaped by past experiences, these patterns have a quiet yet powerful influence on how we perceive the world and interact with those around us. For instance, if someone grew up experiencing constant disapproval, they might instinctively put up their defenses whenever they receive feedback—even if it's meant to be helpful. On the other hand, someone who has always sought approval might go out of their way to chase praise, sometimes losing touch with their true self in the process. Have you ever observed this behavior in others, or perhaps in you at times?

Tying this back to what we explored about judgment in the last chapter, these patterns often thrive on assumptions. We judge the feedback we hear as an attack or the praise we crave as the only measure of our worth. But what if those judgments aren't entirely accurate? What if they're just stories our minds have crafted based on old experiences?

If we look closer, the feedback focuses on the behavior or performance we implemented. Still, somehow, we misattribute that feedback from our past performance to our self-worth, judging who we are rather than laser-focusing on how we performed so we can improve next time.

4.2 How to Identify Emotional Patterns

To identify your emotional patterns, start by paying closer attention to your reactions. Set aside a few minutes each day to write about situations where you experienced strong emotions. Create an emotional pattern journal so you can analyze your patterns:

- Column 1: Write down the strong emotions that you experienced
- Column 2: Write down the circumstances of what was happening
- Column 3: Write down your immediate response
- Column 4: Write down what you were thinking in the moment

Over time, patterns will emerge, revealing why you tend to respond the way you do in specific situations so that you can choose different responses thoughtfully.

Another way to identify patterns in your behavior is to ask others how they see you in various circumstances throughout your workday. Their input could provide valuable insight. Trusted colleagues, friends, or mentors may notice tendencies that you might not recognize in yourself. Their perspective can help you better understand how your emotional responses affect your interactions.

Figuring out where these patterns come from isn't just about understanding the past—it helps you take control of how you act in the present. Maybe the way you react started because of something that happened long ago, like an experience that left a big impression on you or a time you felt hurt or scared. Once you identify where these feelings originated, you can stop letting them control you.

Instead of reacting the same way, you can pause and decide how to handle things. Thoughtful consideration helps you build better relationships, feel more in charge of your emotions, and stay calm when things get tough. Understanding the root of your reactions enables you to grow and make fundamental changes in your life.

4.3 The Impact of Emotional Patterns

When left unexamined, emotional patterns can control your behavior in ways that limit your potential. Consider a manager who consistently reacts defensively to feedback. Over time, this habit can strain professional relationships, prevent personal growth, and damage the manager's reputation.

In contrast, recognizing and addressing these patterns can lead to positive change. For example, a defensive manager could learn to pause and listen more openly to feedback, transforming criticism into an opportunity for development. Similarly, a leader who avoids confrontation could work on being more assertive, improving team dynamics, and building trust. Recognizing and understanding emotional patterns is key to building self-awareness, giving you the tools to handle feedback and professional challenges with greater clarity and confidence.

4.4 Strategies for Changing Emotional Patterns

Once you've identified the patterns that aren't serving you, the next step is to work on changing them. Change takes intention and practice, but it's possible with consistency. One effective method is cognitive reframing, where you challenge negative thoughts and replace them with more constructive ones. For example, if you view criticism as a personal attack, you can reframe it as an opportunity to gain insight and improve.

Self-regulation techniques, such as deep breathing, can help you stay grounded in stressful circumstances. When faced with an emotional trigger, taking a few deep breaths can allow you to choose a thoughtful response rather than an automatic reaction.

Support systems like guided workshops or personal coaching can provide a space to untangle emotional patterns and build new ways of responding to life's challenges. While self-reflection can be helpful and encouraged, there are times when we may be too close to our own experiences to see them. No matter how unhelpful they feel now, old habits and emotional patterns likely made sense at some point in your life. They got you this far, but they can also keep you stuck. If you find yourself spiraling around the same issue and can't seem to overcome it, it may be helpful to ask for help. Having someone skilled to guide the process helps you see what you might otherwise miss.

Sometimes, what we need most is an outside perspective—a mirror that reflects not just what's obvious, but what lies beneath. Whether group or 1-on-1, a skilled partner in this kind of work doesn't just point out patterns; they help you explore them safely and judgment-freely. They might ask, "When did you first start reacting this way?" or "What's underneath this feeling?" Questions like these gently invite you to look deeper, uncovering how your current reactions may be tied to experiences you've long left unexamined. Once you understand where these patterns come from, you're no longer bound by them. That awareness opens the door to responding differently and intentionally.

This kind of guidance doesn't involve criticism or finding fault—it encourages discovery. It creates space for you to see yourself more clearly and build the life you want to lead. When someone helps you connect the dots between old emotional habits and the person you would like to become, it's easier to step away from automatic reactions and start responding in ways aligned with your goals and values.

The real benefit of working with someone this way is the transformation that occurs when you feel seen, understood, and supported. Instead of feeling stuck in the same frustrating patterns, you gain tools to handle situations with an enhanced perspective and confidence. You break free from what's holding you back, and in the process, you learn how to navigate life's challenges with purpose and ease, knowing you've already started rewriting the script of how you respond.

4.5 Emotional Regulation in High-Stress Situations

Stress often manifests when we're faced with high-stakes or high-pressure situations. It arises as a physiological response within your body, where the brain perceives a threat and swiftly prepares the body to either confront it or flee from it. In modern life, these "threats" are rarely physical but rather psychological and emotional, especially in professional environments—whether it's stepping up for a crucial presentation, navigating a tense meeting, or beating a tight deadline.

Have you ever faced a challenging conversation at work and found yourself wondering—whether real or imagined—if your response might put your job at risk? What feelings showed up? Perhaps a burning sensation all over? Maybe nervousness? Did you begin to perspire or experience a rapid heartbeat as your thoughts raced frantically? Or have you ever been in a relationship where a difficult conversation could either bring your partner closer or push them away, all depending on how you choose to respond?

To navigate these high-stress scenarios effectively, it's essential to first pinpoint your specific stress triggers. Are they tied to performance, such as a fear of public speaking or pressure to perform a task? Or are they linked to interpersonal dynamics, like managing conflicts or meeting the expectations of others? Identifying these triggers can empower you to manage and mitigate their impact before they escalate proactively.

Grounding techniques are invaluable tools during acute stress. By focusing on your breathing or the physical sensations of your body, like the feel of your feet on the floor, you can pull your mind away from the stressor and back to the present.

Additionally, adjusting your internal dialogue can significantly influence your emotional state. What are you saying to yourself internally? The layers of judgment that we apply in our thoughts also intertwine closely with our stress levels. Without realizing it, our internal critic can often amplify stress by imposing merciless judgments on our performance or decisions. Judging ourselves without compassion compounds the stress we experience and clouds our judgment further, creating a cycle that is difficult to break.

Check in with yourself during a high-stress situation by asking, "Am I judging this situation as too hard or too difficult? Am I judging myself as not good enough to overcome it?" Identify those judgmental thoughts. As they form, check in with your body to see how they impact your emotions and overall feelings. From there, reframe those judgmental thoughts from "I can't handle this" to "I'm equipped to tackle this challenge." To take reframing a step further, permit yourself to make the reframe even more accurate so that it rings true and feels right. You can say, *"With my training and experience, I am equipped to tackle this challenge as I take in deep, slow breaths and allow my mind to calm. With clarity and peace of mind, the answer shows up."* Not only does this reframe reduce stress, but it also enhances your effectiveness in the situation as the reframe feels more believable.

Shifting towards a mindset of compassion and understanding towards ourselves and others can significantly lighten this emotional load. Initially, it can feel awkward and uncertain. However, by practicing reframing in areas where our inner critic judges us the most and replacing those judgments with observational language, we alleviate stress and create a more constructive and safe space to operate within, ultimately enhancing our capacity to handle high-pressure situations with grace and effectiveness.

4.6 Letting Go of Expectations for Inner Peace

Expectations are a double-edged sword. They can inspire us to strive for something greater but also weigh us down with frustration when things don't turn out as planned. This is especially true at work, where we often expect promotions, recognition, or specific outcomes —and feel deflated when reality doesn't align with our goals.

Letting go of rigid expectations doesn't mean you should lower your standards. Instead, it requires that you shift your focus to what you can control and remain open to possibilities beyond what you envisioned. Refocusing isn't giving up; it's about making space for peace and flexibility in how you respond to life.

So, what are the things we *can* control? Primarily our actions, our efforts, and our perspective. For instance, while you can't control whether your director notices your hard work, you can control the quality of the work you deliver and how you advocate for yourself. Similarly, you can't dictate how others react to your ideas, but you can approach each interaction with clarity and confidence.

Refocusing your attention on what's within your power is where practicing mindfulness and acceptance becomes powerful. Mindfulness is the art of fully being present in the moment—paying attention to what's happening without judgment. It helps you notice when your mind drifts toward "what ifs" or unhelpful assumptions, allowing you to gently bring it back to the present.

Acceptance doesn't mean resigning yourself to whatever happens. Instead, it's about recognizing reality as it is rather than fighting it. When you practice acceptance, you acknowledge that things may not go as planned—and that's okay. Accepting life as it comes, even when things don't go according to plan, creates emotional resilience, so setbacks don't derail your inner peace.

A helpful exercise is to journal your expectations. Write down what you're hoping for and ask yourself:

- Are these expectations realistic, or am I holding on to something beyond my control?
- If this doesn't happen as I envision, what's the next best step?

Reflecting on your answers can help you untangle unnecessary stress and shift your focus to what truly matters. By letting go of rigid expectations, you free yourself to embrace life as it comes—and sometimes, the unexpected outcomes turn out to be precisely what you need.

4.7 Empowering Language for Emotional Mastery

The words we use, both out loud and in our thoughts, profoundly shape how we feel and behave. Negative self-talk, such as "I can't handle this," can chip away at confidence, fuel anxiety, and foster a sense of helplessness. Take a moment to observe how such language makes you feel—tightness in your chest, heaviness in your mood, or a sense of being stuck.

In contrast, empowering language like "I'm capable of figuring this out" can reinforce a sense of control, optimism, and possibility. How does that shift in language feel in your body? Lighter? More expansive? Can you detect the difference? Here's the real question: in both circumstances, who is creating how you feel? I'll give you one guess.

Start by paying close attention to the language you use during challenging situations. Often, small tweaks can make a big difference. Replace "I have to" with "I get to," turning obligation into opportunity. Shift "I can't" into "I'll give it my all," inviting effort and determination instead of defeat. These adjustments might feel subtle, even trivial, at first, but over time, they can profoundly transform your approach to challenges and your overall mindset.

For instance, imagine you're faced with a tight deadline at work. Instead of saying, "There's no way I'll get this done," try, "This is a chance to push my limits and see what I'm capable of." Or in a personal situation, replace, "I'm just not good at this" with, "I'm still learning, and that's okay." Notice how these shifts not only change the tone of your thoughts but also how you feel emotionally and physically.

The power of language lies not in what it says—but in what it creates. With practice, you'll find yourself feeling more resilient, optimistic, and in control, even when life feels uncertain. These small, intentional changes pave the way for meaningful growth in your mood, well-being, and ability to handle life's challenges.

4.8 Building Resilience Through Mindfulness

Resilience helps us navigate the inevitable ups and downs of life—it's the steady anchor that keeps us grounded when the waters get rough. While setbacks and change are unavoidable, how we face them often determines the toll they take on us. This is where mindfulness becomes a daily practice worth highlighting as a preventive measure for stress.

We've touched on mindfulness before, but it's worth emphasizing again because it does more than help you cope in the moment. Daily mindfulness can strengthen your ability to handle stress before it even arrives. Think of it as a muscle that gets stronger the more you use it. When you integrate mindfulness into your daily routine, you're building a reservoir of calm and clarity that you can draw from during high-pressure situations at work or in life.

Mindfulness is the practice of cultivating an awareness of your thoughts, emotions, and physical sensations without judgment. This awareness creates a pause between what happens to you and how you respond. Imagine a tense meeting where emotions are running high. If you've practiced mindfulness, you're less likely to react impulsively —snapping at a colleague or letting your frustration show—and more likely to approach the situation with measured calm.

But the real power of mindfulness lies in its preventive benefits. By spending even five minutes a day on mindfulness techniques like body scans, where you sense how each part of your body is feeling, deep breathing, or gratitude journaling, you train your brain to handle stress differently. Over time, these practices rewire your stress response so that you're less likely to feel overwhelmed or blindsided when challenges arise.

For example, consider deep breathing. When you practice it consistently, your body learns to associate the act of breathing deeply with relaxation. So, in a moment of crisis—like a last-minute deadline or unexpected criticism—your body already knows how to calm itself. Similarly, gratitude journaling helps shift your focus from what's going wrong to what's still going right, fostering resilience through perspective.

Think of mindfulness as a daily tune-up for your mind. Just as you wouldn't wait for your car to break down before getting an oil change, mindfulness works best when it's part of your routine, not a last resort. By incorporating it into your day—whether during a quiet moment with your morning coffee or in the middle of a hectic after-noon—you're creating a mental buffer that makes the inevitable bumps in the road feel more manageable.

In the end, resilience is about building the inner strength to navigate difficulties. By consistently practicing mindfulness, you're not just reacting to stress—you're proactively preparing yourself to handle life's challenges with grace and clarity.

For many professionals, success often feels tied to accomplishments—what you've done, the goals you've hit, and the problems you've powered through. The world usually tells us to push through, no matter how we feel, leading some to see emotions as a sign of weakness or distraction. But here's the truth: learning to understand and manage your emotions doesn't weaken you—it gives you an edge. It's like unlocking a superpower that enhances your skills and achievements.

When you apply the strategies we've covered—like recognizing emotional triggers, practicing mindfulness, and regulating your responses—you don't just manage your emotions better; you amplify your ability to lead, connect, and thrive. For those already excelling, emotional intelligence helps you go even further, proving that you don't need to have it all or be perfect to achieve extraordinary results. People are drawn to you more when you are a leader who excels with effort, even if you don't always get it right, because it makes you relatable. As you allow others to see you both win and experience setbacks, including how you handle them with emotional intelligence, you will inspire many who aspire to improve.

On the other hand, if emotions sometimes dominate your workday, causing you to dwell too much on frustrations or anxieties, balancing them can help you stay more focused on the task. Emotions don't have to control the narrative. When balanced with thoughtful action, they become a guiding force rather than a hindrance.

Rather than ignoring emotions, self-management helps you embrace and align them with your actions to create resilience and strength. By developing this balance, you'll find greater confidence and a more profound sense of fulfillment in your professional and personal journey. With practice, you'll see that emotional intelligence is a path to thriving in every part of your life.

5. Social Awareness: Understanding Others

At the core of every meaningful interaction is the ability to see beyond words—to truly understand the emotions and motivations that shape people's behavior. Think back to a hectic day at work, when you walked into the office, visibly upset about something and missing your usual spark. Imagine if instead of rushing past the moment, your manager stopped, acknowledged your unspoken distress, and checked in with you to see how you were doing. How would that make you feel? That slight pause demonstrates empathy's quiet yet transformative power—a skill that turns routine exchanges into opportunities for connection and growth.

In today's workplaces, empathy is a foundational skill for effective leadership and meaningful collaboration. Leaders who practice empathy can anticipate their team's needs, address challenges with compassion, and inspire loyalty. For example, an empathetic manager might notice a team member struggling and offer support before burnout sets in. These leaders build trust because they see people as individuals, not just roles. Research shows that empathetic workplaces often experience higher engagement, lower turnover, and better decision-making—a compelling case for prioritizing empathy in your daily professional life.

To understand why empathy is so impactful, it helps to unpack the difference between empathy and sympathy. Sympathy often means feeling pity or sorrow for someone else's situation—it's a reaction from the outside, where you acknowledge their struggle but maintain some emotional distance. It can sometimes come across as well-meaning but disconnected, like saying, "That sounds tough," without truly engaging with the deeper emotions behind the situation.

Empathy, on the other hand, takes it a step further. It requires effort and intention, asking you to step into someone else's shoes and experience their perspective as if it were your own. It moves beyond recognizing what someone is going through to truly feel with them and understanding their emotions in a way that fosters connection. For example, instead of simply acknowledging a colleague's frustration over a missed deadline, empathy allows you to imagine how you'd feel in their position—what the stress or disappointment might mean to them personally.

This subtle but powerful shift creates space for authenticity, trust, and respect. When you lead with empathy, you strengthen relationships. You show your team that their feelings matter and that you're willing to see the world through their eyes. These connections transform groups of individuals into cohesive, high-performing teams that work together toward shared goals. Empathy is a strategic advantage in today's workplace.

Interactive Element: Empathy Assessment Exercise

Take a moment to reflect on recent interactions where empathy played a role. Consider the following prompts: How did you respond to someone in need of support? What assumptions did you make, and how did they influence your response? Use these reflections to identify areas for growth and practice empathy in future interactions.

Empathy is more than a skill to be developed; it is a lens through which we view the world. It enriches our understanding of others and enhances our ability to lead and collaborate effectively. As you cultivate empathy, you foster a more inclusive and supportive environment, paving the way for meaningful connections and successful outcomes.

5.1 The Empathy Framework: Five Steps to Perspective-Taking

Here's a practical five-step framework for perspective-taking to help you master empathy for others. This approach helps you actively work to understand them and respond thoughtfully.

Step 1: Notice The Other Person's Disposition

Empathy starts with paying attention. Look beyond the surface and notice changes in mood or behavior. Is your colleague quieter than usual? Are they avoiding eye contact or snapping at small things? Maybe their posture seems slumped, or their enthusiasm has dipped. These cues often signal unspoken emotions. The goal here is observation, not assumption—stay curious and open to what you see.

Step 2: Reflect on Possible Stressors

Once you've noticed their disposition, pause to reflect. Ask yourself open-ended questions. What might be contributing to their emotional state? Consider stressors both inside and outside of work. Maybe they're overwhelmed by a looming deadline or struggling with a tense team dynamic. Or perhaps they're dealing with personal challenges like family responsibilities or health concerns. How often have we made judgments and accusations because we did not take the time to discover the whole story? Reflection helps you approach their situation with a compassionate curiosity to listen and help instead of judging them.

Step 3: Acknowledge Your Assumptions and Biases

Let's be honest—we all carry biases and assumptions. Maybe you've labeled your colleagues "lazy" because they missed a deadline or "difficult" because they pushed back in a meeting. Acknowledging these snap judgments doesn't mean you're a terrible person; it means you're self-aware. Write them down or mentally name them. Identifying your biases is the first step to removing self-imposed barriers toward seeing the person more clearly.

Step 4: Challenge Your Assumptions

Once you've identified your assumptions, ask yourself:

- What might I be overlooking that could help me understand this situation more fairly?
- What else could be happening in their world that I haven't considered yet?
- What would I feel if I were in their shoes?

Challenging your assumptions isn't always easy—you must let go of the "story" you've created about someone and replace it with genuine curiosity. This mindset shift is at the heart of empathy.

Step 5: Consider Time Constraints and Make Empathy Actionable

Time is often the biggest roadblock to empathy, especially in fast-paced environments. But empathy doesn't require hours; it requires intention. If you're short on time, focus on small but meaningful actions. A simple "How are you doing today?" or "I noticed you seemed stressed—can I help?" goes a long way. To make empathy sustainable, look for moments in your schedule where you can slow down and connect. Then, schedule the check-in so that it becomes prioritized.

Why The Empathy Framework Works

This five-step framework—notice, reflect, acknowledge, challenge, and consider—breaks empathy into manageable, actionable pieces. It gives you the tools to navigate emotional dynamics at work with clarity and confidence.

When you approach relationships this way, you're not just reacting to emotions but proactively building trust and strengthening your team. Over time, these steps become second nature, equipping you to handle even the most challenging interpersonal situations with grace and understanding. In turn, you're creating a workplace where everyone feels seen, valued, and supported. And when you do that, you'll find that empathy doesn't just benefit others; it transforms you, too.

5.2 Reading Non-Verbal Cues and Body Language

In the workplace, what goes unsaid often matters as much as—or more than—what's said aloud. Non-verbal cues like body language, tone of voice, and facial expressions reveal emotions and intentions that words may not. Imagine a colleague in a meeting who says they're "fine" but avoids eye contact and fidgets with their pen. Those subtle signals tell a deeper story—perhaps stress or unease.

To interpret these cues accurately, pay attention to context and details. Eye contact, for example, often indicates confidence or engagement, while avoidance might suggest discomfort. Posture can signal someone's mood—a straight posture conveys confidence while slumping might reveal exhaustion or disengagement. The tone of voice, too, carries weight; a hesitant tone may reflect uncertainty, even if the words express agreement.

But be cautious. Cultural differences can influence how people use and interpret non-verbal cues. For instance, maintaining eye contact may be respectful in some cultures but intrusive in others. Similarly, personal space preferences and gestures vary widely, which can lead to miscommunication. The key is to approach non-verbal communication with cultural awareness and adaptability.

To hone your skills, engage in role-playing exercises where you and your colleagues practice interpreting body language in different scenarios. Silent activities, like charades or non-verbal storytelling, can sharpen your ability to read gestures and expressions. Feedback from peers during these exercises will enhance your awareness, making you more adept at navigating the unspoken dynamics of workplace interactions.

5.3 Active Listening: Beyond Words

Listening is one of the most underrated tools in professional communication. It's easy to assume we're listening when we're just waiting for our turn to talk. Active listening requires being fully present and engaged, not just hearing words but understanding the message and emotions behind them.

To practice active listening, start with simple yet powerful techniques. Paraphrase what the speaker has said to confirm your understanding and show that their words matter to you. Ask open-ended questions to encourage deeper dialogue. Nonverbal feedback, such as nodding your head or maintaining eye contact, signals your attentiveness. In the workplace, where misunderstandings can lead to missed opportunities or mistakes, these techniques reduce confusion and build trust.

Distractions are a common barrier to active listening. Whether it's the constant ping of notifications or a racing to-do list, losing focus is easy. Combat this by creating distraction-free environments for meaningful conversations—put your phone away, close your laptop, and give the speaker your full attention. Recognize when your mind wanders and gently refocus on the person before you.

More than just a polite gesture, active listening helps people form meaningful connections. In customer service, for instance, attentive listening can turn frustrated clients into loyal advocates. In team settings, it fosters collaboration and helps uncover innovative solutions. By making active listening a habit, you'll enhance your professional relationships and ability to lead with empathy.

The CLEAR Framework for Active Listening

Consider the acronym CLEAR (Center, Listen, Echo, Ask, Respond) to put active listening into a strategic framework.

1. **Center Yourself.** Before engaging in a conversation, mentally prepare to be fully present. Silence your phone, close unnecessary tabs on your computer, and take a deep breath to reset your focus. Ask yourself: What does this person need from me right now—my attention, advice, or understanding? This sets the tone for a meaningful and undistracted exchange.
2. **Listen Fully.** Give the speaker your undivided attention. How? Maintain steady eye contact, nod occasionally to show engagement, and lean slightly forward to signal interest. Avoid interrupting or formulating your response while they're still talking. Instead, focus on their words, tone, and body language to fully absorb their message.
3. **Echo Their Message.** Paraphrase or summarize what you've heard to confirm your understanding. For example:
   - **"So I'm hearing that the deadline feels tight because of competing priorities—does that sound right?"**
   - This ensures clarity and shows the speaker that their thoughts are valued and respected.

4. **Ask Thoughtful Questions.** Use open-ended questions to encourage the speaker to elaborate and dig deeper into the issue. For instance:
   - **"Can you tell me more about what's been most challenging for you this week?"**
   - **"What do you think would make this process easier for the team?"**
   - These questions demonstrate genuine curiosity and help you uncover details that might not surface otherwise.

5. **Respond with Care.** Once the speaker has finished, respond thoughtfully and constructively. Avoid jumping straight to solutions unless they're explicitly asking for them. Instead, acknowledge their perspective with empathy:
   - **"I can see why this has been frustrating. Let's figure out how we can tackle it together."**
   - This approach promotes collaboration and reassures the speaker that they've been heard and understood.

5.4 Cultural Sensitivity in Emotional Intelligence

As workplaces grow increasingly diverse, cultural sensitivity has become paramount in emotional intelligence. Every culture expresses emotions and interprets behavior through its lens, shaped by values, norms, and traditions. Understanding these nuances is essential for building trust and inclusivity in multicultural environments.

To develop cultural awareness, start with education. Attend cultural competence training or explore resources highlighting different customs and communication styles. Engaging with colleagues from varied backgrounds—through conversations, community events, or shared projects—provides firsthand insights into their experiences. Within your team, encourage open dialogue about cultural diversity to deepen mutual understanding and create a more inclusive environment.

Be mindful of the challenges, though. Stereotypes and unconscious biases can cloud your perceptions, leading to missed opportunities for genuine connection. Commit to self-reflection and question assumptions you might hold. When in doubt, ask thoughtful questions instead of making assumptions—this shows respect and encourages more transparent communication.

For example, instead of assuming someone celebrates a specific holiday, you could ask, "What holidays are meaningful to you?" I've worked with someone whose family migrated to the United States, who does not celebrate Christmas. Meanwhile, everyone else on the team did celebrate the Christmas holiday. At first, the team reacted with shock. Their initial assumption was, "Who doesn't celebrate Christmas or want to participate in the Secret Santa gift exchange?" However, the teammate stood firm on her views of why she doesn't celebrate Christmas, sharing her culture and her values of what is most important to her. She also reassured them verbally that their gift exchange would not offend her nor make her feel left out. With time, they came to accept her position, ultimately expanding their awareness of cultural differences.

If you're curious about someone's perspective, try, "What has been your experience with this?" When collaborating, ask, "Is there a different approach you'd recommend based on your experience?" These kinds of questions demonstrate genuine interest and allow for deeper, more meaningful conversations that honor diverse perspectives.

By embracing cultural sensitivity, you enhance your emotional intelligence and ability to navigate today's global workplace complexities. Teams that value diverse perspectives work more cohesively and generate more innovative ideas. As you embrace cultural sensitivity in your interactions, you'll discover its power to deepen connections and unlock new growth opportunities.

To be socially aware means recognizing the humanity in those around you. Paying attention to subtle expressions, asking thoughtful questions, and embracing diverse perspectives allows you to foster trust and mutual respect in any setting.

Make a Difference with Your Review
Unlock the Power of Generosity

"We rise by lifting others"

— *Robert Ingersoll*

Giving a little can mean a lot. Your kindness can brighten someone's day—and maybe even change their life.

Would you help someone like you—someone curious about emotional intelligence but unsure where to begin?

My mission is simple: to make understanding and mastering emotional intelligence easy, practical, and life-changing for everyone.

But here's the truth: most people pick a book based on reviews. That's why I need your help. Your review could make all the difference.

Imagine how your review could help someone:

- Feel more confident at work and build better relationships.
- Manage their stress and stay calm under pressure.
- Communicate with clarity and connect with others more deeply.
- Become the leader others look up to and respect.

It takes less than a minute, but your words could guide someone on their journey to mastering their emotions and transforming their life.

Ready to help? Simply scan the QR code below or click this link:

👉 [https://www.amazon.com/review/review-your-purchases/?asin= B0DSPW3J1D]

Thank you for taking the time to support this mission. Your kindness matters more than you know.

With gratitude,

Kevin L. Goins

6. Relationship Management: Building Strong Connections

Trust is one of those things you can't hold in your hands, but its presence—or absence—is unmistakable. It's what gives people the confidence to work together effortlessly, turning a group of individuals into a unified team. When trust exists, you see it in the way people share ideas freely, support each other, and take risks without worrying about judgment. Without it, everything feels harder—conversations become guarded, defensiveness takes over, and the team's momentum slows to a crawl.

After a corporate merger, the workplace often feels like unfamiliar territory. Roles are shuffled, processes evolve, and uncertainty hangs heavy in the air. People start wondering where they fit, what's expected of them, and whether their contributions will still matter. It's a fragile time when emotions run high, and the environment can foster growth or deepen divisions.

In one department, you can feel the tension. Team members hold back, reluctant to share ideas, fearing they'll be dismissed or judged. Meetings are quiet, not because everyone agrees, but because no one feels safe enough to speak up. Collaboration becomes transactional—just enough to get by—while real innovation stalls. The team isn't just dealing with change; they're navigating it in isolation, and the cracks begin to show.

Contrast that with another department led by someone who understands the importance of trust. Here, questions aren't seen as challenges; they're invitations to explore solutions. Concerns are met with openness, not defensiveness, creating an atmosphere where people feel heard. Even mistakes are treated as stepping stones for growth, rather than moments to assign blame. Team members don't just work together—they trust each other to have their backs.

What sets these two teams apart isn't the merger or the workload—it's trust. In one team, the lack of trust has created a cautious, disconnected group where every interaction feels like a risk. People are more focused on protecting themselves than contributing fully. In the other team, trust acts as a bridge, allowing individuals to lean on one another, share openly, and tackle challenges as a unified group.

Trust is the backbone of meaningful relationships at work and in life. It doesn't happen by chance—it's built through consistent actions, clear communication, and emotional intelligence. In teams where trust is prioritized, you'll find a culture where creativity flourishes, collaboration becomes second nature, and people are genuinely invested in each other's success. When trust is strong, the workplace shifts from a place of mere tasks to a space where people feel valued and connected, no matter what challenges arise.

Interactive Element: Trust-Building Exercise

Consider incorporating trust-building activities into your team meetings to strengthen connections. Try a simple icebreaker where each member shares a personal story or experience that taught them the value of trust. You can guide the activity by offering a prompt, such as "Describe a time when someone placed trust in you and how it impacted you." Afterward, reflect as a group on common themes or insights that emerge. This exercise encourages vulnerability and openness, laying the groundwork for more profound trust and collaboration within the team.

In both professional and personal settings, trust is the cornerstone of successful relationships. By understanding its importance and employing strategies to build and maintain it, you can create an environment where connections are strong, resilient, and enduring.

6.1 The Foundations of Trust

At its heart, trust is the belief that others will act with reliability, integrity, and goodwill. It is the pillar of every successful relationship, both professional and personal. Within teams, trust creates the psychological safety needed for members to share ideas, provide honest feedback, and work towards common goals without fear of betrayal or judgment. This openness unlocks creativity and collective problem-solving.

Contrast this with low-trust teams: conversations feel guarded, collaboration stalls, and creativity is stifled. Distrust breeds suspicion and defensiveness, creating an environment where even the simplest tasks become cumbersome. The difference between a high-trust and low-trust team is stark, and its impact on performance is undeniable.

6.2 How Emotional Intelligence Builds Trust

Emotional intelligence (EI) lays the groundwork for trust by helping us navigate relationships with empathy, authenticity, and fairness. It involves more than just kindness or understanding—it helps create an environment where people feel safe to be themselves, knowing they won't be judged or dismissed.

Take empathy, for example. As we discussed earlier, empathy is central to understanding others, and here, we see it come full circle as a building block of trust. It's one thing to notice when a team member seems stressed, but it's another to respond with genuine care. A manager who says, "I see you've been under a lot of pressure—how can I support you?" practices empathy and lays the groundwork for trust. Rather than attempting to solve all their problems, the goal is to show them that that their feelings matter and that they're valued as a person.

What makes this approach so effective is the absence of judgment. Contrast it with a dismissive response like, "You need to get it together," which can break trust instantly. Instead, empathy invites connection, creating a safe space where trust can grow—something we know is vital to strong, lasting relationships.

Judgment, whether subtle or overt, can erode trust faster than you realize. It creates a barrier that keeps people from opening up, sharing ideas, or asking for help. Emotional intelligence helps us replace judgment with curiosity, encouraging us to see situations through another person's lens. This shift makes room for understanding, even when you don't fully agree or have all the answers.

But empathy alone isn't enough—again, trust also hinges on consistency. It's easy to say the right things, but it's your actions that prove reliability. When your words align with what you do, you build a track record of integrity. For instance, if you promise to address a concern raised in a meeting, following through shows your team that you mean what you say. Over time, this consistency reassures people that they can count on you, whether it's for small commitments or larger challenges.

Emotional intelligence amplifies trust by guiding how you navigate these dynamics. It helps you check your biases, manage your reactions, and stay intentional about creating connections. When you lead with EI, you're not just managing tasks—you're building relationships where trust becomes second nature, opening the door to deeper collaboration and a stronger sense of belonging.

The TRUST Framework: Building Connections That Last

To help you build and maintain trust, here's a simple yet powerful framework you can apply:

T – Transparency

Open communication is the bedrock of trust. Share information honestly, even when it's difficult. When team members understand the "why" behind decisions, they're more likely to buy into the process. For example, instead of withholding details about an organizational change, explain its rationale and potential impacts.

R – Respect

Show respect through active listening and validation. Respect doesn't mean agreeing with everything; it means acknowledging the other person's perspective as valuable. Ask yourself, *"How can I make them feel heard and understood?"*

U – Understanding

Empathy lies at the heart of understanding. Take the time to consider what someone might be experiencing, both at work and beyond. For example, if a colleague misses a deadline, reflect on possible stressors instead of jumping to conclusions.

S – Support

Demonstrate your commitment by offering help and encouragement. Whether it's delegating responsibilities to show trust or simply checking in, small actions build a foundation of support.

T – Tenacity

Building trust isn't a one-time effort; it requires persistence, especially during tough times. Show tenacity by sticking to your commitments, addressing issues head-on, and consistently reinforcing trust through action. Perseverance in maintaining trust demonstrates that it's a priority, even when circumstances get challenging.

Practical Steps for Building Trust

1. Listen actively
   - Pay full attention when someone speaks, paraphrase to confirm understanding and ask thoughtful follow-up questions. This strongly suggests that you value their input and care about their perspective.
2. Demonstrate consistency in words and actions
   - Always align your actions with your promises. For example, if you commit to addressing an issue, make it a priority to follow through.
3. Encourage vulnerability
   - Create spaces for open dialogue where team members feel safe sharing concerns. Vulnerability fosters connection and demonstrates that trust goes both ways.
4. Celebrate wins together
   - Acknowledge team achievements regularly. Recognizing contributions reinforces the idea that success is a shared effort.

6.3 Why Trust Matters: Examples

High-trust environments drive exceptional outcomes. Take the example of a project manager leading a high-stakes initiative. By prioritizing open communication, offering consistent support, and addressing team concerns transparently, she built a culture where trust thrived. The result? Her team not only met tight deadlines but also exceeded expectations, empowered by a sense of shared purpose and connection.

Similarly, in personal relationships, trust is transformative. Consider a couple navigating a disagreement over shared responsibilities. One partner feels overwhelmed by managing household tasks, while the other believes they are contributing enough. Tensions escalate as resentment grows on both sides, and communication becomes increasingly strained.

Without trust, this disagreement can spiral into defensiveness, criticism, and emotional distance. However, with intentional use of empathy and active listening, they have the opportunity to rebuild trust and strengthen their bond.

How do they use empathy and active listening?

- Each pauses and reflects on their feelings and needs. In a safe space reserving judgment, each gets to share how they feel.
- They agree to schedule a time to talk with each other. Even if they do not agree, they agree to listen and validate each other's feelings openly.

By practicing empathy and active listening, they can rebuild trust and find common ground, strengthening their bond in the process.

Interactive Element: Trust-Building Exercise

Strengthen trust in your team with this simple yet impactful exercise:

The "Trust Story" Circle

1. Gather your team in a casual setting.
2. Ask each member to share a brief personal story about a time when trust played a pivotal role in their success or growth.
3. Reflect as a group on the themes that emerge, such as vulnerability, accountability, or empathy.

This activity encourages openness and demonstrates the universal value of trust, laying the groundwork for stronger connections.

Trust turns uncertainty into opportunity. It's the quiet force that anchors relationships during challenges and propels them to new heights in collaboration and connection. Incorporating the TRUST framework into your leadership goes beyond strengthening connections—it creates an environment where people feel safe, valued, and inspired to do their best work together.

7. Emotional Intelligence in the Workplace

If you've been following this book, you've already explored the transformative power of emotional intelligence (EI) across teams, leadership, and workplace dynamics. So why dedicate another chapter to the topic? Because what I have come to understand is that EI in the workplace is more than a concept to understand—it's a toolkit to master. Each aspect of EI we've discussed so far builds to this point, where it all converges into actionable strategies for navigating complex relationships, fostering team collaboration, and advancing your career.

This chapter connects the dots in new, innovative ways. Instead of simply revisiting earlier ideas, you will learn how to apply them with fresh insight. How does EI unlock creativity in team settings? What role does it play in building trust through inclusion? How can leaders use emotional agility to enhance their presence and influence? And perhaps most importantly, how can you wield these skills to navigate office politics and shape your career? Let's get into it.

7.1 Emotional Intelligence in Team Dynamics

The way people interact within a group has a profound impact on how they collaborate and achieve goals. These interactions show up in the sharing of ideas, handling of disagreements, and the sense of value each person feels they bring to the group. The focus shifts from getting tasks done to influencing how individuals connect, communicate, and navigate challenges together. At the heart of all this is emotional intelligence (EI), the skill that turns these interactions into meaningful and productive teamwork.

Building emotional intelligence within a group is the foundation for creating trust and psychological safety. These aren't abstract concepts; they're what make people feel comfortable enough to share ideas without fear of being judged or dismissed. For example, introducing something as simple as a "roundtable" discussion during meetings, where everyone has a chance to speak without interruptions, can completely change the dynamic. It ensures everyone feels heard and valued, building a culture of inclusion and respect.

Emotional intelligence is about understanding and managing emotions as they arise, both in yourself and others. For example, when tensions rise during a discussion, someone with strong emotional intelligence can sense the shift, acknowledge it, and help steer the conversation back to a constructive place. Activities like empathy mapping, where you take time to see a situation from another person's perspective, can make a huge difference. It allows you to understand not just what someone's words but the meaning behind them.

When people feel understood and valued on this level, collaboration moves to a whole new level. The focus shifts from completing tasks to creating a team environment where everyone feels respected, connected, and empowered to bring their best ideas forward. Emotional intelligence is what makes this possible.

7.2 Enhancing Executive Presence Through Emotional Agility

Executive presence is often described as the elusive "X-factor" that sets great leaders apart. It's the ability to project confidence, inspire trust, and command respect in a way that feels authentic and approachable. For those looking to step into leadership roles, executive presence is the bridge between competence and recognition. For those already in leadership, it determines whether people see you as a leader worth following.

Contrary to popular belief, executive presence isn't defined by charisma alone—it's rooted in substance, strategy, and self-awareness. It's how you show up in the room, handle challenges, and connect with others. At its core, executive presence is deeply tied to emotional agility—the ability to navigate your emotions and adapt your responses without losing focus or composure.

7.3 Why Emotional Agility is Key

Think about the leader who handles a project crisis with poise. Instead of reacting impulsively—blaming the team or panicking— they take a moment to assess the situation, acknowledge the effort that's already been made, and calmly outline a path forward. That measured response solves the immediate issue while simultaneously reassuring the team that they're in capable hands. Emotional agility enables this kind of response. It allows leaders to manage their emotions effectively, even in high-pressure situations, and project the calm authority that inspires confidence.

For aspiring leaders, developing emotional agility is essential for building credibility. Although you might already have the skills and expertise for the next step in your career, executive presence signals to others that you're ready to lead. For those already in executive roles, emotional agility ensures that your leadership doesn't falter under pressure or alienate your team.

7.4 Executive Presence in Action

Let's break down the components of executive presence to see how they come to life:

1. **Gravitas: The Weight of Leadership**
   - Gravitas is what gives your leadership authority. It's not a matter of being louder or dominant. Gravitas is found in how you carry yourself and how you handle critical moments. Leaders with gravitas demonstrate steadiness under pressure. For example, in a contentious boardroom discussion, a leader with gravitas doesn't get easily rattled. Instead, they listen actively, respond thoughtfully, and maintain a calm demeanor that commands respect.
   - To cultivate gravitas:
     - Practice pausing before responding in tense situations. This shows you're measured and intentional.
     - Seek feedback on how you handle high-stakes moments and refine your approach.
2. **Communication: The Power of Connection**
   - Communication is the thread that ties executive presence together. It's not just about what you say but how you say it. Strong communicators know how to tailor their message to their audience, whether they're inspiring a team, presenting to stakeholders, or rallying a crowd.
   - For example, consider a leader addressing a team after a difficult quarter. Instead of focusing solely on the negatives, the leader acknowledges the challenges but shifts to a vision for the future, using personal stories or data points to make the message resonate.
   - To enhance communication:
     - Practice active listening to truly understand your audience's concerns before you speak.
     - Develop your storytelling skills to make your messages more relatable and memorable.

3. **Authenticity: The Foundation of Trust**
    -   People trust genuine leaders. Authenticity is the ability to align your actions with your words and your values. Leaders who try to be someone they're not often come across as insincere, which undermines their credibility.
    -   Authenticity doesn't mean oversharing—it means being transparent about your intentions and consistent in your behavior. For instance, if you ask your team for feedback, show you're willing to act on it. Authentic leaders inspire trust because their teams know what to expect from them.
    -   To build authenticity:
        -   Reflect on your core values and ensure your decisions align with them.
        -   Be open about your strengths and areas for growth—it humanizes your leadership.

4. **Emotional Agility: The Glue That Holds It Together**
    -   Emotional agility ties gravitas, communication, and authenticity together to create a cohesive presence. Without it, even the best intentions can falter. Leaders who lack emotional agility may become reactive, let their emotions dictate their behavior, or struggle to connect with others during tough times.
    -   For example, imagine a leader whose frustration with a missed deadline spills over into a meeting. Their tone becomes sharp, and the team withdraws instead of engaging. Contrast this with a leader who acknowledges their disappointment calmly and refocuses the discussion on solutions. The second leader's emotional agility transforms the situation into an opportunity for growth.
    -   To develop emotional agility:
        -   Use mindfulness techniques, like deep breathing or pausing before reacting, to regulate emotions in the moment.

- Journal about emotionally charged situations to identify triggers and develop strategies for managing them.
- Role-play challenging scenarios to practice maintaining composure.

5. **Appearance: The Visual Message You Send**

   o While appearance isn't the most important factor in executive presence, it undeniably plays a role in shaping first impressions. The way you present yourself visually—your attire, grooming, and body language—can either reinforce or detract from your credibility as a leader.

   o Consider a leader walking into a high-stakes meeting. Their outfit is polished but not flashy, their posture exudes confidence, and their demeanor signals that they're prepared. This attention to detail aligns their appearance with the seriousness of the occasion, creating an impression of professionalism and respect for the setting.

   o Appearance is less about following rigid dress codes and more about aligning your outward presentation with your personal brand and organizational culture. For example, in a creative field, your attire might reflect innovation and individuality, while in a corporate environment, a more formal approach may be expected.

   o To refine your appearance:
     - **Dress with intention.** Choose clothing that fits the context and sends the right message about who you are as a leader.
     - **Mind your posture.** Standing tall and maintaining open, confident body language communicates self-assurance.
     - **Pay attention to grooming.** Small details—like clean shoes or a well-groomed appearance—can subtly enhance how others perceive you.

Your appearance isn't about vanity; it's a demonstration of respect—for yourself, your role, and the people you're leading. When your outward presentation aligns with your values and professionalism, it amplifies the other elements of your executive presence.

For the Aspiring Leader

If you're aiming for a promotion, think of executive presence as your calling card. In addition to possessing the technical skills, you must demonstrate to others that you can handle the responsibility and represent the organization effectively.

I remember earlier in my career, I applied for a manager position while still on probation. Two other candidates who applied worked there for 9 years before my start. When the decision was made, I got the promotion.

The interviewers told me that I had two key advantages over the others, which were the deciding factors in my favor. Number one was how I showed up dressed for the interview; I appeared serious to the interviewers. The second thing was my ability to communicate a clear vision for working with over two hundred individuals—many of whom would be shocked that I was promoted because of my newness with the company—while also developing a strategic vision for the department to exceed its targets. I had read 65 books on how to lead others the year prior and attended four leadership conferences to beef up my skills.

The interviewers worried about two potential situations with the other two candidates. Their biggest concern was whether or not the candidates would still act as friends with the employees they once lunched with should they get promoted. Also, should the situation call for it, would they be able to make the tough decisions concerning discipline? In other words, did they show they could handle the responsibility despite their 9-year technical tenure over mine?

Start by focusing on how you present yourself in meetings, handle feedback, and build relationships with your peers. Each interaction is an opportunity to exhibit gravitas, communicate clearly, and build trust.

For the Established Executive

If you already hold a leadership role but feel your presence isn't where it should be, focus on alignment. Are your actions reflecting your values? Are you consistent in how you show up for your team? Remember, executive presence isn't about perfection—it's about intention. Take time to refine your emotional agility, strengthen your communication, and seek feedback from trusted colleagues to identify blind spots.

The Impact of Executive Presence

Whether you're working toward a leadership role or trying to refine your effectiveness as an executive, enhancing your executive presence pays dividends. It's the difference between being competent and being compelling. It's the reason people turn to you in a crisis, trust your vision, and rally behind your leadership.

By cultivating gravitas, sharpening your communication, staying true to your values, and building emotional agility, you create a presence that inspires others and strengthens your ability to lead effectively. Executive presence is much more than a skill—it's a strategic advantage worth developing.

7.5 Navigating Office Politics with Emotional Intelligence and a Lens of Judgment

Office politics often evokes feelings of frustration or hopelessness, leading many to quit rather than face the challenge. Yet, the unique perspective of emotional intelligence (EI) allows us to reframe office politics as an opportunity for growth. By examining the role of judgment vs. observation, we can better understand the dynamics of perceived and active politics and adopt strategies that promote connection and clarity instead of disconnection and conflict.

Office politics can take two forms: perceived politics, where we sense something is amiss but lack concrete evidence, and active politics, where the maneuvering is overt and undeniable. While both scenarios are challenging, judgment often worsens the situation. When we assign meaning to situations too quickly—filling in the gaps with assumptions—we risk misunderstanding the dynamics entirely. Recognizing and managing judgment is key to navigating these complexities effectively.

Perceived Politics: Navigating Uncertainty

The Role of Judgment in Perceived Politics

Perceived politics thrive in environments where information is scarce or ambiguous. You notice a manager favoring certain team members, a closed-door meeting, or a coworker's sudden shift in demeanor, and judgment kicks in: *"They're probably talking about me."* This automatic conclusion is your brain's shortcut, based on incomplete data and shaped experiences. But these snap judgments often lack the full context and can lead to unnecessary stress or alienation.

The antidote? Shifting from judgment to observation. Instead of labeling behaviors, approach them with curiosity. For instance, instead of thinking, *"They're playing favorites,"* you might observe, *"The manager meets with those team members often."* This shift removes emotional charge and allows you to ask clarifying questions or seek additional context without defensiveness.

Framework: The ASK Model for Perceived Politics

To navigate perceived politics while avoiding the pitfalls of judgment, use the **ASK** model:

- **A – Acknowledge Your Feelings**
  - Recognize how the uncertainty makes you feel—whether it's suspicion, anxiety, or frustration. Validating your emotions allows you to manage them instead of being controlled by them.
- **S – Seek Facts, Not Assumptions**
  - Pause and ask: *What do I actually know for sure?* Separate what's observable (e.g., meetings are happening) from what's assumed (e.g., they're plotting against me).
- **K – Keep Communication Open**
  - Engage in conversations that clarify rather than fuel assumptions. For example, you might say, *"I noticed there's been a lot of discussion about the project. Is there anything I can do to contribute?"* This opens a door for transparency and builds trust.

Active Politics: When the Game Is Real

The Role of Judgment in Active Politics

In active politics, the maneuvering is visible, and the impacts are tangible. You might see credit being stolen, alliances forming, or exclusionary behavior developing. When on the receiving end, judgment can amplify feelings of resentment or victimization. For example, you might think, *"They're out to get me,"* instead of observing, *"They've aligned themselves with leadership."* This judgment often leads to emotional reactions that escalate the situation, such as withdrawing or reacting defensively.

Switching to observational thinking empowers you to respond strategically. Instead of taking actions personally, you can analyze behaviors through the lens of motivation: *"What might be driving their behavior? How can I navigate this constructively?"*

Framework: The PATH Method for Active Politics

To handle active politics with clarity and emotional intelligence, follow the **PATH** method:

- **P – Pause and Reflect**
  - Before reacting, take a moment to process. What are you observing, and how does it make you feel? This step helps prevent reactive decisions and allows for thoughtful responses.
- **A – Analyze Motivations**
  - Consider what might be driving the political behavior. Is someone vying for recognition? Protecting their position? Understanding these dynamics helps you depersonalize the situation.
- **T – Take Strategic Actions**
  - Decide on your next steps based on observation, not judgment. This might include documenting your contributions, building alliances with trusted colleagues, or seeking mentorship to navigate the landscape.
- **H – Hold Your Integrity**
  - Stay true to your values, even in a challenging environment. Engage in transparent, ethical communication, and resist the urge to stoop to political tactics that undermine trust.

7.6 Why People Quit and Why They Shouldn't

Many professionals consider leaving their jobs when faced with office politics, driven by feelings of frustration, helplessness, or burnout. While quitting may seem like the easiest way to escape, it often robs you of the chance to grow. Navigating office politics with emotional intelligence—and using frameworks like **ASK** and **PATH**—gives you the tools to manage these dynamics effectively and emerge stronger.

By addressing judgment and practicing observational thinking, you:

- Break the cycle of assumptions that fuels stress.
- Foster healthier relationships with colleagues.
- Empower yourself to respond strategically rather than react emotionally

7.7 The Role of Emotional Intelligence in Office Politics

EI allows you to see office politics not as a threat, but as a challenge to rise to with confidence and integrity. It helps you regulate your emotions, understand the motivations of others, and build the relationships needed to thrive. When judgment is replaced with observation, and reaction is replaced with strategy, you gain control over your response to office politics, no matter how complex.

Office politics doesn't have to be a dead end. With the right mindset and tools, it can become an opportunity to grow your influence, build resilience, and strengthen your professional relationships. Instead of jumping ship, learn to navigate the waters. You might find that the journey makes you a more effective, emotionally intelligent leader

7.8 Emotional Intelligence in Performance Reviews

Performance reviews often provoke anxiety, but with EI, they become opportunities for connection and growth. The key is to approach them as conversations, not critiques.

Start with empathy. Before the review, reflect on the employee's recent work and challenges. During the meeting, begin with open-ended questions like, "How do you feel about your progress this quarter?" This invites self-reflection and shows that you value their perspective.

Provide balanced feedback by highlighting strengths before discussing areas for improvement. Use specific examples to ground your observations. For instance, instead of saying, "Your communication needs work," try, "In the last meeting, I noticed some of your points got lost. Let's explore ways to make your ideas stand out more."

Finally, set clear, actionable goals. Employees should leave the review not just knowing where they stand but also feeling equipped to grow.

7.9 Leveraging Emotional Intelligence for Career Advancement

If you've been applying emotional intelligence (EI) in your professional life, you've already taken a step ahead of the pack. While EI is crucial for navigating relationships, it's also a tool for personal growth and career advancement. One of the most impactful ways to leverage EI for promotion and recognition is by building a personal brand.

Many people misunderstand what a personal brand is, equating it to social media profiles or flamboyant self-promotion. In reality, your personal brand is the reputation you cultivate—the consistent impression others have of your skills, values, and personality. It's reflected in the way you show up, interact, and add value every day. And the good news? EI can help you craft a brand that is authentic, compelling, and aligned with your career goals.

7.10 How to Build a Personal Brand with Emotional Intelligence

Think of your personal brand as the answer to this question: *What do I want to be known for?* Here's a step-by-step guide to help you intentionally build it:

1. **Define Your Core Values and Strengths**
   - Your brand starts with understanding yourself. Reflect on your core values, strengths, and unique selling points. These are the foundation of your brand and guide how you want to be perceived. Ask yourself:
     - What do I care about most in my work? (e.g., innovation, collaboration, excellence)
     - What emotional intelligence strengths set me apart? (e.g., empathy, adaptability, conflict resolution)
     - What impact do I want to have on others? (e.g., inspiring trust, fostering creativity, driving results)
   - Write these down and use them as your "brand pillars." For instance, if empathy and problem-solving are your strengths, aim to be seen as a leader who resolves conflicts and brings teams together.

2. **Align Actions with Intentions**
   - Your brand isn't built on what you say—it's built on what you do consistently. Every interaction, decision, and project is an opportunity to reinforce your personal brand. For example:
     - If collaboration is part of your brand, seek out cross-functional projects and highlight your ability to unite diverse teams.
     - If professionalism is key, show up on time, meet deadlines, and communicate clearly.
     - If emotional intelligence is your strength, be the person who defuses tension and models empathy, even in challenging situations.
   - Consistency is crucial. If your actions don't align with your stated values, your brand will come across as inauthentic.

3. **Make Your Strengths Visible**
   - Doing great work is just one part of your brand. Ensuring the right people notice it is equally important. This doesn't

mean bragging or self-promotion; it means strategically showcasing your contributions. Here's how:

- **Document Your Wins**: Keep a running list of achievements, from projects you've led to conflicts you've resolved. Be ready to share these in performance reviews or networking conversations.
- **Speak Up in Meetings**: Share insights and ideas that reflect your expertise and values. Your voice is a key part of your brand.
- **Share Credit Generously**: Recognizing others' contributions shows humility and collaboration—both hallmarks of an emotionally intelligent brand.

4. **Seek and Act on Feedback**
   - High-EI professionals understand that feedback is a gift. It's also essential for shaping your personal brand. Regularly ask trusted mentors, peers, or supervisors how you're perceived and where you can improve. Questions like:
     - *What do you think I'm best known for in the team?*
     - *Are there areas where I could show up more effectively?*
     - This feedback helps you identify blind spots and fine-tune your brand.

5. **Network Authentically**
   - Your brand extends beyond your immediate team or department. Networking allows you to expand your reach and build relationships that align with your career goals. Use EI to network with intention:
     - **Focus on Relationships, Not Transactions**: When meeting someone new, prioritize curiosity. Ask about their work, goals, or challenges. For example, *"What's been the most rewarding part of your role lately?"* Genuine interest builds trust and lasting connections.
     - **Offer Value First**: Networking isn't just a way to ask for help—it's also a chance to offer it. Share a resource,

connect someone with a contact, or simply offer a kind word of encouragement.

6. **Craft Your Professional Narrative**
    ◦ Your personal brand is more than a collection of traits—it's a story. What's the overarching narrative you want others to associate with you? For example:
        ▪ *"I'm someone who thrives in high-pressure situations by staying calm, listening to all perspectives, and finding solutions that benefit everyone."*
        ▪ Share this narrative in subtle ways, like weaving it into conversations, LinkedIn profiles, or personal introductions.

7.11 Why Personal Branding Matters for Career Advancement

Whether you're aiming for a promotion or looking to make a career shift, your personal brand acts as your professional reputation. It tells decision-makers what you bring to the table and why they should trust you with greater responsibilities. By leveraging emotional intelligence, you ensure that your brand is not just authentic but also impactful.

For someone early in their career, this approach helps build credibility and opens doors. For an established professional, it reinforces your leadership and influence. Either way, to craft your personal brand, you need to climb the ladder and make sure you leave a meaningful mark at every step. Your personal brand is already forming every day—make it intentional, make it authentic, and let EI guide the way.

In conclusion, this chapter is more than a continuation of the book's themes—it's a call to action. Emotional intelligence in the workplace isn't just about understanding others; it's about using that understanding to create impact. Whether you're leading a team, navigating office dynamics, or charting your career path, EI equips you with the tools to succeed.

8. Emotional Intelligence in Leadership

Leadership transcends the mechanics of task management and goal-setting. At its essence, it revolves around connecting with people, understanding their motivations, and steering through challenges with vision and purpose. Emotional intelligence (EI) amplifies this connection, transforming leadership into a force that shapes cultures, drives results, and establishes the emotional heartbeat of teams and organizations.

To lead with EI means understanding that people are at the core of every decision, strategy, and outcome. Leadership requires a skillful balance of directing workflows or hitting metrics, fostering trust, creating a shared vision, and navigating a team's emotional complexities. In this chapter, we'll explore how EI reshapes leadership through emotion-centered connection, informed decision-making, and culture-building. We'll also introduce the **LEADER Framework**, a practical guide to embedding emotional intelligence into your leadership style.

Interactive Element: Emotional Intelligence Reflection Section

Take a moment to reflect on your own leadership style. Consider the following prompts: How do you currently incorporate emotional intelligence into your interactions? What areas can you develop to better connect with your team? Identify one actionable step you can take this week to enhance your emotional intelligence in leadership. This reflection will help you build on the insights shared in this chapter, paving the way for deeper connections and more effective leadership.

8.1 Emotion-Centered Leadership

Leading with emotion means moving past simple management to truly inspire those you guide. It recognizes that emotions drive behavior, and by understanding these emotional undercurrents, leaders can unlock their team's full potential. Leaders with high EI create emotional resonance, forging connections that motivate people to align their personal goals with the organization's mission.

The Core Principles of Emotion-Centered Leadership

1. **Understand Before Leading**
   - Emotion-centered leaders prioritize understanding their team's needs, fears, and motivations. Rather than simply asking what a team member needs to succeed, the leader focuses on truly listening and observing their emotional cues. For example, if a team member seems disengaged, an EI-driven leader might ask, *"What's been on your mind lately?"* instead of making assumptions about their performance.
2. **Model Emotional Transparency**
   - Authenticity builds trust. Leaders who appropriately share their own emotions set the tone for openness. When a leader admits, *"I'm feeling a bit uncertain about this change,*

but I'm confident we'll figure it out together," they show vulnerability without undermining their authority, fostering a culture of honesty.

3. **Foster Emotional Safety**
   - Emotional safety means creating an environment where team members feel comfortable expressing concerns or ideas without fear of judgment. This safety encourages creativity and collaboration, as team members know their input is valued.

The LEADER Framework

To embody emotion-centered leadership, use the LEADER framework as a guide:

- **L – Listen Actively**
  - Practice deep listening, focusing on what's said and unsaid. Show you value their voice.
- **E – Empathize Genuinely**
  - Seek to understand team members' emotions and perspectives. Ask, *"How can I support you?"*
- **A – Align Goals**
  - Connect team members' personal aspirations with the organization's objectives.
- **D – Demonstrate Transparency**
  - Share appropriate emotions and challenges to model openness and trust.
- **E – Empower Your Team**
  - Provide the tools, autonomy, and encouragement they need to succeed.
- **R – Reinforce Positivity**
  - Celebrate wins, recognize contributions, and create an environment of optimism.

Embracing the LEADER framework means adopting a mindset where leadership is driven by trust, integrity, and meaningful connections.

8.2 Emotional Intelligence and Decision-Making in Leadership

Decisions define leadership. Whether you're guiding a team through change, resolving conflict, or setting a long-term strategy, your ability to make sound decisions is the foundation of your effectiveness. EI brings a unique edge to decision-making by blending emotional awareness with logic and data, ensuring that choices resonate with both people and objectives.

Balancing Emotion and Logic

Great leaders know that effective decisions prioritize people, not just numbers. For instance, a cost-cutting measure might make financial sense but devastate team morale if handled insensitively. EI helps leaders anticipate and manage these emotional impacts, ensuring decisions are both effective and empathetic.

Practical Application: Before implementing a decision, ask yourself:

- *"How will this affect team dynamics?"*
- *"What emotions might this decision evoke, and how can I address them?"*

Recognizing Emotional Bias

Even the best leaders are susceptible to biases like overconfidence or fear of failure. These emotions can cloud judgment, leading to impulsive or overly cautious decisions. EI allows leaders to pause and reflect, ensuring their choices are balanced and thoughtful.

Practical Application: When you sense a bias, step back and ask:

- *"Am I making this decision based on facts, or am I letting my emotions take over?"*
- Seek input from a trusted colleague for a fresh perspective.

Using Emotional Awareness to Drive Better Outcomes

Emotions provide context to decisions, revealing how choices will be received by those affected. Leaders with EI can anticipate resistance, adapt their approach, and communicate decisions in a way that fosters understanding and support.

Practical Application: Incorporate emotional risk assessments into your decision-making process. For example, consider:

- *"How will this change impact morale? What steps can I take to ease the transition?"*

By integrating EI into decision-making, you ensure that your leadership is both strategic and human-centered.

8.3 Building a Culture of Emotional Intelligence

Leadership doesn't stop with individual influence—it extends to shaping the broader organizational culture. A workplace rooted in EI fosters innovation, collaboration, and loyalty. When employees feel valued and understood, they bring their best selves to work, driving both personal and organizational success.

Steps to Build an EI-Centric Culture

1. **Train and Develop EI Skills**
   - Invest in workshops and training programs to equip employees with emotional intelligence tools.

- Example: A company introduced empathy-building workshops during onboarding, setting the tone for collaboration from day one.

2. **Embed EI in Policies and Practices**
   - Make emotional intelligence a measurable part of performance reviews, hiring processes, and leadership evaluations.
   - Example: An organization revamped its performance review system to assess not only technical skills but also emotional competencies such as teamwork and adaptability.

3. **Lead by Example**
   - Leaders set the tone for an EI-focused culture. By modeling empathy, transparency, and active listening, they inspire employees to do the same.
   - Example: A healthcare CEO held regular open forums to listen to employee concerns, creating a culture of trust and inclusion.

8.4 Case Studies: Leadership in Action

Consider these examples to illustrate the profound influence of EI in leadership.

The Innovator

The CEO of a growing tech startup noticed her team struggling creatively under the weight of tight deadlines and mounting pressure. Understanding how crucial emotional intelligence is in leadership, she chose to take action. She introduced regular brainstorming sessions where everyone felt safe to share ideas—no matter how out-of-the-box they seemed. This simple yet impactful step sparked new ideas, while also building a culture of respect and trust. Over time, the team's creativity rebounded, morale soared, and they rediscovered their ability to tackle challenges together. It was a powerful reminder of how emotional intelligence can transform a workplace and unlock innovation.

The Crisis Manager

During a tough merger, a senior leader made empathy and open communication his top priorities. He started holding daily check-ins with his team, giving everyone a chance to voice their concerns and feel heard. By showing he truly cared and staying transparent, he kept morale high and built trust when it mattered most. His approach helped the team navigate the transition smoothly and stay united through the challenges.

The Mentor

An engineer with a strong technical background found it difficult to connect with her team. Determined to improve, she worked on building her emotional intelligence by practicing active listening and learning how to give thoughtful feedback. Over time, she became a trusted mentor, gaining her team's respect and creating a more collaborative, supportive environment.

8.5 Reflection and Next Steps

Take a moment to consider your own leadership style. How do you currently integrate emotional intelligence into your decisions and interactions? What is one step from the LEADER Framework you can implement this week to strengthen your connection with your team?

Leadership is defined by progress, not perfection. By cultivating emotional intelligence, you can inspire trust, foster collaboration, and drive success with authenticity and purpose. Let EI be the foundation of your leadership legacy.

9. Stress Management, Combating Burnout, and Emotional Flexibility

S tress is an inevitable part of life, especially in high-pressure environments. But what if the way we interpret stress holds the key to managing it? Much of the tension we feel doesn't stem from external circumstances but from how we *judge* those circumstances. When we label situations as overwhelming or impossible, we amplify the pressure and create emotional turmoil. Shifting from judgment to observation can be transformative, reducing stress by allowing us to see challenges more clearly and respond with greater calm.

Here's something you might not have considered: while stress may start as an emotional burden, it also has a tangible impact on your physical health, including your weight. Chronic stress triggers the release of cortisol, a hormone designed to help us survive immediate threats. However, when stress becomes a constant, cortisol remains elevated, leading to cravings, fat storage (especially around the abdomen), and even weight gain over time. How many of us unknowingly contribute to our own stress—and potentially our own stubborn body fat—simply by how we judge situations?

Have you noticed by now how hard it is to avoid the negative impacts of judgmental thinking? Can you see how our choices in thinking, judging, or observing tend to creep into so many things that we do and experience? Are you beginning to understand the importance of recognizing judgmental thinking as "the untrained brain" and the art of observational thinking is like saying "the trained brain"? Reflect on it as you begin to see overlapping patterns throughout the book.

This chapter explores the powerful connection between stress, mindset, and the body. It shows you how to control your stress responses for better emotional and physical well-being.

Interactive Element: Stress Level Assessment

Consider keeping a stress diary for a week. Note situations that trigger stress, your emotional and physical responses, and the outcomes. Reflect on patterns and identify areas for improvement. This exercise will give you a clearer picture of your stress landscape and guide you toward more effective management strategies.

For example, imagine you're stuck in traffic on your way to work, and it triggers stress. In your stress diary, you might write:

- **Situation:** Heavy traffic made me late for work.
- **Emotional Response:** Frustration, anxiety about being late.
- **Physical Response:** Tight chest, clenched jaw, headache.
- **Outcome:** I arrived at work feeling irritable and distracted.

After a week, you notice a pattern: traffic delays consistently trigger stress, affecting your mood throughout the day. To improve, you decide to leave home earlier to avoid rush hour or listen to calming podcasts during your commute to stay relaxed.

In this fast-paced world, where demands are constant and expectations high, the ability to transform stress into productivity is a skill that sets successful individuals apart. By understanding the nuances of stress and employing practical techniques, you can unlock your potential and achieve personal and professional fulfillment.

9.1 Understanding Stress Through Observation

Stress is often misunderstood and perceived as an entirely negative force. But not all stress is harmful. Certain stress levels can actually be motivating—this is known as eustress, the "positive stress" that challenges us to grow and perform at our best. Unlike distress, which leaves us feeling overwhelmed and stuck, eustress energizes us, sparking creativity, focus, and achievement.

Think about a moment when you were preparing for an important presentation or working against a tight deadline. That rush of adrenaline, the heightened sense of urgency—it wasn't debilitating. Instead, it pushed you to focus, prioritize, and bring your best ideas to the table. This is eustress in action: it sharpens your mind and fuels productivity by creating just enough pressure to ignite motivation without tipping into overwhelm.

The key difference between eustress and distress often lies in how we interpret what's happening around us. With eustress, challenges are viewed as opportunities to stretch our limits, learn, and grow. Distress, on the other hand, emerges when we see challenges as insurmountable threats. For example, facing a new role at work might feel daunting. Through the lens of eustress, you might think, *"This is a chance to expand my skills and prove what I can do."* In contrast, distress might lead to thoughts like, *"I'll never be able to handle this—it's too much."*

This difference in interpretation is where judgment versus observation plays a significant role. Judgment amplifies distress by turning challenges into self-criticism: *"I'm not good enough for this"* or *"I'm going to fail."* Observation shifts the narrative, allowing you to see the facts without emotional weight: *"This is a challenging project, but I have the resources and time to figure it out."* By reframing how we perceive stress, we can harness the empowering energy of eustress and prevent it from spiraling into distress.

9.2 The Role of Judgment in Stress

Judgment amplifies stress because it attaches emotion and meaning to circumstances. When we judge a situation, we often add layers of self-criticism or fear, turning simple challenges into overwhelming problems. This emotional attachment intensifies our stress response, making it harder to think clearly or take productive action. Shifting from judgment to observation allows us to approach situations with a calmer, more solution-focused mindset.

For example, seeing a full inbox might lead to thoughts like, *"I'm failing at staying on top of things,"* which spikes anxiety. Observation removes the emotional charge, letting you see it neutrally: *"There are 50 unread emails, so I'll prioritize the most urgent."* This shift creates clarity and reduces cortisol-triggering reactions.

But here's a deeper layer: every time you engage in judgment-driven stress, you might also be fueling weight gain. When stress triggers cortisol—your body's primary stress hormone—it signals the brain to seek comfort, often in the form of high-calorie, sugary, or fatty foods. This is a biological response designed to store energy during perceived threats, and it poses a real threat to your willpower. Unfortunately, when cortisol levels stay elevated due to chronic stress, it can lead to increased cravings, overeating, and the accumulation of abdominal fat, which is particularly harmful to long-term health.

By shifting your mindset from judgment to observation, you calm your emotional response and give your body a chance to reset. Imagine noticing a stressful situation like a missed deadline and responding with "This happened; I'll focus on what I can do next" instead of "I'm terrible at managing my time." This subtle change reduces the cortisol spike, helping you avoid the cycle of stress-induced cravings and weight gain. Could practicing this shift ease your stress and improve your physical health over time? The connection between mindset and body might be stronger than you think.

The STRESS Framework for Managing Mindset

To reduce stress and cortisol levels while fostering an observational mindset, try the STRESS framework:

- **S – See the Situation Clearly**
    - Identify what's happening without attaching labels like "good" or "bad." Focus on facts, not feelings.
- **T – Take a Moment to Pause**
    - Before reacting, pause to breathe and reset. This prevents knee-jerk responses fueled by emotion.
- **R – Reframe the Challenge**
    - Shift your perspective by asking, *"What can I learn or gain from this situation?"*
- **E – Engage with the Present**
    - Use grounding techniques like conscious breathing or the "5-4-3-2-1" method to focus on the now.
- **S – Seek Support**
    - Share your concerns with a trusted colleague or friend to gain perspective and reduce isolation.
- **S – Strategize Your Next Steps**
    - Break tasks into manageable pieces and focus on actionable solutions.

This framework helps you transition from reacting emotionally to responding thoughtfully, reducing stress and its physical impacts.

9.3 Combating Burnout Before It Takes Hold

Burnout doesn't happen overnight. It creeps in gradually, often fueled by prolonged stress, overwhelming responsibilities, and unaddressed emotional strain. You might start noticing small signs—difficulty focusing, constant fatigue, or a growing sense of irritability—but brush them off as temporary. Left unchecked, these signals can snowball into full-blown burnout, characterized by emotional exhaustion, detachment from work or relationships, and a sharp decline in productivity.

However, burnout doesn't have to be inevitable. It starts with awareness. Recognizing the warning signs early gives you the power to address them before they escalate. Prioritize small but meaningful steps like setting boundaries, carving out time for rest, and reconnecting with activities that energize you. By taking deliberate action, you can protect your well-being, reignite your passion, and maintain the energy needed to navigate life's demands. Remember, self-care isn't selfish—it's essential for long-term resilience.

Recognizing Burnout

Burnout often manifests as:

- Persistent fatigue that no amount of rest alleviates.
- Emotional detachment or cynicism about work.
- A noticeable decline in performance and motivation.

Consider this: If burnout begins with stress, and stress amplifies through judgment, how might shifting your perspective impact your trajectory? Could reframing how you see challenges stop burnout before it starts?

Strategies to Prevent Burnout

1. Set Boundaries
   - Establish clear limits for work hours and personal time to protect your mental and emotional health.
2. Delegate and Prioritize
   - Avoid taking on everything at once. Focus on high-impact tasks and seek help when needed.
3. Engage in Restorative Activities
   - Spend time on activities that rejuvenate you, whether it's exercising, meditating, or connecting with loved ones.
4. Seek Support Early
   - Open conversations with supervisors or colleagues about workload challenges, which can lead to collaborative solutions.

9.4 Awareness-Based Strategies for Stress Reduction

Awareness is the antidote to stress. It allows you to step back, observe your emotions, and create space between what's happening and how you choose to respond. Instead of being swept away by the emotional intensity of a situation, awareness gives you the tools to approach it with a clear, steady mind. This practice doesn't eliminate stress but helps you manage it more effectively, turning reactive moments into thoughtful, intentional ones.

Focusing on the present moment is key. Techniques like mindfulness encourage you to tune into your surroundings and let go of distractions, while breathing exercises help calm your nervous system by lowering your heart rate and signaling safety to your brain. For example, try the 4-7-8 technique: inhale for four seconds, hold for seven, and exhale for eight. Sensory grounding is another powerful tool—notice five things you can see, four you can touch, three you can hear, two you can smell, and one you can taste. These small yet impactful practices anchor you in the now, breaking the cycle of spiraling stress and fostering clarity and calm.

The beauty of awareness is that it's always available, no matter where you are or what you're doing. Whether it's pausing before a difficult conversation, taking a deep breath during a tense moment, or simply observing the sensations of your body as you sit, awareness empowers you to respond to life's challenges with greater ease and resilience. It's a skill that grows with practice and becomes a cornerstone of lasting well-being.

Techniques to Cultivate Awareness

- Notice thoughts without judgment:
    1. **How to Do It**: Sit quietly and bring awareness to your thoughts and emotions. Pay attention to moments when you label them as "good" or "bad," "right" or "wrong." Instead of criticizing yourself for judging, gently acknowledge the judgment and let it pass, like a wave returning to the ocean.

    2. **Importance**: Recognizing judgment in real-time helps you see how often it shapes your reactions. This awareness creates space to respond thoughtfully rather than react impulsively.
    3. **Benefits**:
        a. Reduces the grip of negative self-talk and criticism.
        b. Builds self-compassion by allowing acceptance of all emotions and thoughts.
        c. Promotes emotional clarity and helps you understand how judgment influences your choices.
- Engage your senses to bring yourself back to the present:
    1. **How to Do It**: Identify 5 things you can see, 4 you can touch, 3 you can hear, 2 you can smell, and 1 you can taste.

2. **Importance**: This technique directs attention to external stimuli, pulling you out of a cycle of overwhelming thoughts.
3. **Benefits**:
   a. Interrupts rumination or panic.
   b. Enhances mindfulness by engaging all senses.
   c. Helps reconnect with your environment.
- Focus on deep breathing with texture focus:
   1. **How to Do It**: Hold an object with texture (e.g., a smooth rock, fuzzy fabric). As you breathe deeply, focus on the feel of the object in your hand.
   2. **Importance**: Combines tactile grounding with breathwork, both of which calm the nervous system.
   3. **Benefits**:
      a. Reduces stress hormones like cortisol.
      b. Increases oxygen flow to the brain, improving clarity.
      c. Promotes a sense of calm and control.
- Use sensory grounding techniques:
   1. Body scan exercise:
      a. **How to Do It**: Slowly focus on each part of your body, starting from your toes and moving upward, noticing any sensations.
      b. **Importance**: Redirects attention inward to neutral, physical sensations rather than overwhelming emotions or thoughts.
      c. **Benefits**:
         - Releases tension stored in the body.
         - Promotes self-awareness and emotional regulation.
         - Encourages relaxation by activating the parasympathetic nervous system.
   2. Visual Anchoring
      a. **How to Do It**: Look closely at a specific object, like a plant or a piece of art. Notice its colors, shapes, and details.

    b. **Importance**: Visual focus shifts your attention outward, reducing internal chaos.

    c. **Benefits**:
   - Enhances mindfulness by encouraging observation.
   - Reduces feelings of dissociation.
   - Encourages appreciation of the environment.

3. Cold Sensation Reset:

    a. **How to Do It**: Hold a piece of ice, splash cold water on your face, or place a cool object on your wrist.

    b. **Importance**: The cold sensation activates the dive reflex, which slows the heart rate and promotes relaxation.

    c. **Benefits**:
   - Quickly calms overwhelming emotions.
   - Brings focus to physical sensations rather than distressing thoughts.
   - Eases symptoms of panic attacks.

4. Rhythmic Movement:

    a. **How to Do It**: Walk slowly and focus on the sensation of your feet touching the ground, or rock gently in a chair.

    b. **Importance**: Engages proprioception (the sense of body position and movement) to ground you physically.

    c. **Benefits**:
   - Reduces anxiety through rhythmic, repetitive motion.
   - Encourages calm through physical connection to your surroundings.
   - Supports emotional regulation.

By practicing these techniques consistently, two things happen. Number one, you're reducing stress. And number two, you're also actively lowering cortisol levels, which can positively impact your overall health.

9.5 Emotional Flexibility: Adapting to Change with Resilience

In a world of constant change, emotional flexibility truly is a super-power. It's the ability to bend without breaking, to adjust your perspective when life throws you a curveball, and to keep moving forward even when the path feels uncertain. This skill allows you to face obstacles with resilience, turning challenges into opportunities for growth and setbacks into stepping stones toward something better.

But emotional flexibility doesn't involve pretending everything is fine or brushing off your feelings. Instead, it gives you permission to feel—whether it's frustration, sadness, or disappointment—while also having the courage to explore what those emotions are teaching you. For example, if a project at work doesn't go as planned, instead of dwelling on what went wrong, you might ask yourself, "What can I learn from this experience? How can I use this to improve next time?"

Developing emotional flexibility takes practice, and it starts with self-awareness. Pay attention to how you react in moments of stress or uncertainty. Are you rigid in your thinking, or can you step back and see things from another perspective? Small shifts, like reframing a situation or looking for the silver lining, can make a big difference. Over time, you'll find it easier to adapt gracefully, bouncing back from challenges with a sense of purpose and clarity.

In a world that's constantly evolving, emotional flexibility helps you navigate life's ups and downs with confidence and ease. It allows you to embrace change as an opportunity rather than a threat, and reminds you that even the toughest moments can lead to personal growth.

Building Emotional Flexibility

1. Reframe Challenges
   ○ Instead of viewing change as a threat, see it as an opportunity for growth.
2. Practice Self-Compassion
   ○ Treat yourself with kindness during tough times. Acknowledge your feelings without judgment and focus on progress over perfection.
3. Strengthen Support Networks
   ○ Lean on trusted friends, colleagues, or mentors for encouragement and perspective.

The flexibility to adapt emotionally doesn't just help you thrive in uncertain times—it also reduces the physiological impact of stress, contributing to better mental and physical health.

A New Perspective on Stress

Most people think of stress as something purely mental, but its impact on your physical body and overall health is profound. Stress doesn't just weigh on your mind—it manifests in tight shoulders, tension headaches, disrupted sleep, and even weight gain. What's even more surprising is that much of this is within your control. The way you interpret and judge situations can send your cortisol levels soaring, affecting everything from your energy and mood to your metabolism. Imagine being late to an important meeting. Would you think, "I'm failing, this will ruin everything," or could you step back and observe: "I'm running behind, but I can focus on delivering my best when I get there"? That small shift can have a powerful effect on how your body reacts to stress.

What if you could take that step back consistently? Shifting from judgment to observation not only reduces stress but also changes how your body physically responds. You might notice a calmer heart rate, a clearer mind, and even a more balanced appetite. The simple act of noticing without attaching criticism allows you to interrupt the stress response before it spirals out of control.

Becoming aware of your stress triggers is the first step to regaining control, and tools like the STRESS Framework can help you break the cycle of automatic reactions. The focus moves past stress management toward creating a new relationship with stress, where you reclaim your power instead of feeling at its mercy. Think of it like rewiring your mind and body to respond differently: less fight-or-flight and more calm, deliberate action.

The secret isn't in avoiding stress entirely—that's unrealistic. Life will always have its challenges. The real breakthrough comes when you learn to understand your stress, reshape your reactions, and approach life with more clarity and resilience. What would change for you if you made this shift? Would you sleep better, feel lighter, or move through your days with more confidence? The choice is in your hands, and it starts with a single step: awareness.

10. Conflict Resolution and Negotiation

Conflict is a part of life—it's unavoidable and often unpredictable. What truly matters is how we choose to navigate it. Will we let it divide us, or will we use it as an opportunity to build stronger connections? At the heart of effective conflict resolution lies emotional intelligence (EI)—the ability to recognize, understand, and respond to emotions in a way that promotes collaboration rather than division. It doesn't involve avoiding conflict but approaching it with curiosity, empathy, and a willingness to understand.

This chapter builds on the concepts of judgment and observation introduced earlier, diving deeper into how these mindsets play a pivotal role in conflict resolution. When we approach disagreements with an untrained brain, our instinct is often to judge. This can look like assuming the worst about someone's intentions, labeling them as "difficult," or reacting defensively to protect our ego. These judgments escalate tensions and create emotional distance, making it harder to find common ground. In the heat of the moment, our reactive minds can dehumanize others, reducing them to the source of our frustration instead of seeing them as people with their own feelings, needs, and perspectives.

But what if we shifted from judgment to observation? An observational mindset, grounded in emotional intelligence, invites us to pause, step back, and see the situation—and the people involved—more clearly. Instead of assuming, we can ask: "What might they be feeling right now? What's driving their behavior? How can I express my needs without placing blame?" These simple yet powerful questions can transform a heated dispute into a productive dialogue. When we shift from reaction to reflection, from "What's wrong with them?" into "What can we both learn here?"

For example, imagine a colleague dismissing your idea during a team meeting. The instinct to judge might lead you to think, "They never take me seriously," sparking resentment and tension. But an observational approach could help you reframe the situation: "They might be under pressure or have a different perspective. Let me ask for clarification and share why this idea matters to me." This small shift in mindset not only defuses potential conflict but also opens the door for meaningful collaboration.

Emotional intelligence doesn't eliminate conflict; it transforms it. By learning to navigate disagreements with empathy, self-awareness, and open communication, we can turn moments of tension into opportunities for connection and growth. What would happen if, instead of fearing conflict, you saw it as a chance to deepen relationships and build mutual understanding? That's the power of emotional intelligence in action—and it's a skill anyone can develop with practice and intention.

10.1 The Role of Judgment and Observation in Conflict

When conflict arises, the brain's default mode is judgment. This instinct, designed for quick decision-making, often leads us to categorize others into oversimplified labels like "selfish," "incompetent," or "arrogant." These judgments create emotional barriers, but even worse, they also dehumanize, reducing others to "not like us" and making it easier to dismiss their feelings or perspectives. Neuroscience research by Lasana Harris and Susan Fiske (2006) has shown that when people perceive others as fundamentally different, the medial prefrontal cortex (mPFC)—the part of the brain responsible for empathy—shows reduced activity. This response explains why judgmental thinking amplifies emotional distance and blocks resolution.

For example, in a workplace disagreement over a project timeline, a team member judged as "lazy" might be someone struggling with burnout or unclear instructions. However, the brain's untrained instinct focuses on the label, reinforcing division and escalating conflict. This dynamic underscores the importance of emotional intelligence: awareness of these automatic judgments allows us to pause, observe, and approach conflicts with greater understanding.

Interactive Element: Emotional Awareness Checklist

- **Personal Reflection**: Note your initial emotional response to a conflict. Are you feeling defensive or anxious? Recognizing these feelings is the first step in managing them.
- **Observation**: Pay attention to the other person's body language and tone. Are they crossing their arms? Speaking more softly or loudly? These cues can provide insight into their emotional state.
- **Validation**: Acknowledge the emotions involved. A simple statement like, "I can see this is important to you," can defuse tension and show empathy.
- **Open Dialogue**: Encourage the other party to express their feelings and thoughts. Ask open-ended questions to fully understand their perspective.

10.2 Dehumanization: The Science of Emotional Distance

Dehumanization—the process of perceiving others as less than fully human—is an extension of unchecked judgment. Studies like the Stereotype Content Model (SCM) by Susan Fiske reveal that people are unconsciously categorized based on perceived warmth and competence. Those viewed as low in these traits are often dehumanized, leading to diminished empathy and harsher treatment. This psychological distancing can manifest in the workplace as power struggles, miscommunication, or outright disregard for others' needs and well-being.

Judgment, in its initial stages, often feels like a logical assessment—a quick mental shortcut to make sense of another person's behavior. For example, when the marketing team perceives product development as "arrogant," it likely stems from an interpretation of their actions: perhaps product development dismissed their suggestions in a meeting. Similarly, when product development labels marketing as "uninformed," it may come from frustration over perceived gaps in technical understanding. At this stage, judgment begins as an emotional reaction tied to unmet expectations or perceived threats.

However, judgment rarely stops there. When left unchecked, it evolves into a reinforcing loop that solidifies negative perceptions. The marketing team doesn't just describe product development as "arrogant" in one instance—they begin to generalize this label to all their interactions, expecting dismissive behavior even before it occurs. This mental shortcut shifts from being an isolated judgment to a fixed narrative. Once this happens, teams stop seeing each other as individuals with legitimate concerns and instead view the other group as a monolith: "They're always dismissive," and "They never understand us."

This transition from judgment to entrenched perception lays the groundwork for dehumanization. At this point, the other group is no longer seen as a collection of people with their own fears, motivations, and challenges—they are simply "the problem." The marketing team becomes "that arrogant bunch," and product development becomes "those uninformed marketers." These labels strip away individuality and complexity, making it easier to disregard the other group's feelings, perspectives, and contributions. Emotional detachment takes hold, and the empathy required for resolution evaporates.

The longer this pattern persists, the deeper the divisions grow. Teams operate in silos, reinforcing their narratives with selective attention to behaviors that confirm their judgments while dismissing evidence to the contrary. This entrenched mindset fosters a toxic cycle: the more people feel dehumanized, the more likely they are to respond in ways that justify the other side's negative perception. Without intervention, this spiral of judgment and dehumanization makes constructive dialogue nearly impossible.

Emotional intelligence provides the key to breaking this cycle. It allows individuals to recognize these patterns as natural but untrained responses of the brain, not immutable truths. By pausing to understand the journey from initial judgment to dehumanization, we can illuminate the path forward, reclaiming empathy and paving the way for meaningful conflict resolution.

The untrained brain's reliance on judgment isn't a personal failure; it's a survival mechanism evolved to simplify complex social dynamics. However, in modern workplaces, this instinct often creates unnecessary tension. Emotional intelligence transforms this by enabling individuals to shift from judgment to observation, reframing others' behaviors as expressions of unmet needs or differing perspectives. This foundational awareness is the first step toward resolving conflict effectively.

10.3 Emotional Awareness: Understanding the Drivers of Conflict

Conflict often begins with surface-level disagreements—a policy change, a missed deadline, or competing priorities. On the surface, these issues seem straightforward, even trivial at times, but beneath them lie complex emotional currents. The colleague resisting a new policy may appear stubborn, vocalizing concerns that seem irrational or overly critical. However, when we look deeper, we might uncover an emotional driver, such as fear of losing control over their role or anxiety about their ability to adapt to new expectations. Without recognizing these underlying emotions, we risk misinterpreting their resistance as a personal affront or deliberate obstruction.

Consider this scenario: a team introduces a new workflow designed to streamline processes. One team member consistently pushes back, delaying implementation and frustrating others. At first glance, their actions seem rooted in defiance or a desire to maintain the status quo. Colleagues begin to judge them as "resistant to change" or "difficult to work with." These judgments, however, obscure the reality of the situation. The team member might be grappling with a fear of being left behind, worried that the new system will expose a gap in their skills or reduce their relevance in the organization.

When these emotional undercurrents continue unacknowledged, conflict festers. The team's growing frustration with the colleague leads to exclusion from discussions or subtle dismissals of their input, reinforcing the team member's fears and further entrenching their resistance. Both sides dig in, and the original disagreement about the workflow becomes secondary to the interpersonal tensions now driving the conflict.

By failing to address these hidden fears and unmet emotional needs, we allow judgment to dominate our perception. The labels—"stubborn," "unreasonable," "difficult"—become barriers to empathy, preventing us from seeing the situation through the other person's eyes. As the cycle continues, we lose sight of the shared goal that initially brought us together, replacing collaboration with division.

As you reflect on this section, have you ever misjudged a situation or person at work? If so, how did your personal judgment of the person or situation influence your behavior?

10.4 The Judgment-Observation Shift: From Reaction to Understanding

The key to resolving conflicts lies in moving from judgment to observation, as has been stated in many situations and relationships with others throughout the book. Judgment labels others, amplifies emotional barriers, and creates an "us versus them" mindset. Observation, by contrast, reframes behaviors objectively, allowing you to see the facts without assigning blame. For example, instead of thinking, "They're being difficult," you might observe, "They're expressing concerns about how this change affects their workload."

This shift offers more than a mental exercise; it becomes a practice rooted in emotional intelligence. By training your brain to approach conflicts with curiosity rather than defensiveness, you create space for understanding and connection. This observational mindset, rather than focus on eliminating disagreements, it reframes them as opportunities to explore diverse perspectives and find common ground.

10.5 Application: Awareness in Action

Consider a clinical setting where emotions run high and critical outcomes hang in the balance. In a conflict between a hospital's administrative team and its nursing staff, tensions escalate over scheduling policies. The administrators introduced a new shift-rotation system designed to optimize patient coverage. However, the nursing staff pushes back, arguing that the policy creates unpredictable schedules that disrupt their personal lives and lead to burnout.

At first glance, the administrators see the resistance as "unreasonable" and dismiss the nurses as "complainers." Meanwhile, the nurses judge the administrators as "out of touch" and "only focused on numbers, not people." These judgments deepen the divide. Meetings to address the issue turn combative, with both sides fixated on defending their positions. No progress is made, and frustration grows on both ends.

What's really happening here? On the surface, the conflict seems to be about scheduling logistics, but the emotional drivers tell a different story. For the administrators, the new system represents a necessary strategy to meet patient care standards under tight constraints. They might also feel unappreciated for their efforts to solve a complex problem. On the other hand, the nurses' resistance stems not from a dislike of change, but from a deeper concerns: a fear of losing control over their work-life balance, exhaustion, and a sense that their well-being is being overlooked.

This emotional disconnect transforms a solvable issue into a seemingly intractable conflict. Administrators, focused on operational goals, fail to acknowledge the nurses' valid concerns. Meanwhile, the nurses, feeling dehumanized and unheard, escalate their frustration, creating an environment of mutual resentment.

Now, let's introduce emotional intelligence into the equation. Instead of labeling each other as "unreasonable" or "out of touch," both sides take a step back to explore the emotions driving the conflict. The administrators, practicing empathy, recognize that the nurses' concerns are rooted in burnout and the fear of losing personal autonomy. The nurses, in turn, acknowledge the pressure administrators face in balancing patient needs with resource limitations.

Through this shift from judgment to observation, the conversation changes. The nurses express their need for a more predictable schedule to maintain work-life balance, and the administrators share their constraints and goals. Together, they collaborate to tweak the rotation system, finding a compromise that ensures patient care while addressing the nurses' concerns. The result is not only a resolution but also a stronger sense of mutual respect and understanding.

This scenario illustrates how emotional intelligence can transform conflict by uncovering the hidden emotional drivers beneath the surface. When we pause to see beyond judgment and address the underlying fears, needs, and frustrations, we create the conditions for meaningful resolution.

10.6 Closing Reflection

Judgment is a reflex of the untrained brain, a survival mechanism designed to simplify the complex world around us. But in the context of human conflict, this reflex can create unnecessary emotional barriers and dehumanize others, preventing meaningful resolution. By understanding the role of emotional intelligence in shifting from judgment to observation, you empower yourself to navigate disagreements with greater empathy and effectiveness. This awareness is the foundation of mastering conflict resolution, transforming it from a source of division into an opportunity for growth and collaboration.

11. Emotional Intelligence for Personal Growth

Emotional intelligence is pivotal in personal development, offering a pathway to understanding and managing your emotions effectively. This self-awareness allows you to identify your strengths and weaknesses, leading to better decision-making and goal-setting. When you understand what drives your emotions, you can align your personal and professional ambitions more closely with your values and aspirations. This alignment enhances your ability to set and achieve personal goals while also building emotional resilience, that allows you to face challenges with a balanced perspective.

In stressful situations, EI offers strategies for emotional regulation, transforming stress into a catalyst for growth rather than a stumbling block. Effective communication skills emerge as another benefit, improving your interactions and fostering more meaningful connections with others.

Recognizing areas for personal growth is essential for harnessing EI's potential. Stress management is a significant area where emotional regulation plays a crucial role. By learning to manage stress, you gain control over your emotional responses, reducing the impact of stressors and enhancing your overall well-being. Communication skills, too, can be refined through EI. Improved communication enhances your effectiveness in professional settings. The ability to communicate also enriches personal relationships, allowing for more authentic and empathetic interactions. As you identify these areas, you uncover the potential for growth and transformation, paving the way for a more fulfilling life.

11.1 Fostering Emotional Intelligence in Family Dynamics

The foundation of healthy family relationships is emotional intelligence, specifically its ability to strengthen understanding and support. It plays a vital role in creating environments where each member feels valued and heard. In parenting, emotional regulation is crucial because it encourages parents to model patience and empathy, thus showing children how to manage their emotions constructively. When a child throws a tantrum, your calm response teaches them more than words ever could. By maintaining composure, you demonstrate how to handle frustration and disappointment, setting a foundation for their emotional growth. Supporting children's emotional development involves nurturing their ability to express feelings and recognize others' emotions. Encourage them to label their emotions—for example, "I feel sad" or "I'm excited"—helping them build a vocabulary that empowers them to communicate their internal world effectively.

Cultivating emotional intelligence within families requires intentionality and practical strategies. Family discussions offer a platform for open emotional expression. By regularly gathering to talk about highs and lows, you create a safe space for sharing and listening. This practice not only strengthens bonds but also teaches children the value of empathy and communication. Introducing emotional vocabulary early can transform how children interact with the world. Encourage them to articulate their feelings, helping them develop self-awareness and empathy. Simple questions like, "How did that make you feel?"

can prompt reflection and discussion, deepening their emotional understanding.

Family conflicts are inevitable, but emotional intelligence offers tools for resolution and growth. When siblings argue, mediating with empathy helps them see each other's perspectives. Guide them to articulate their feelings and needs, fostering mutual understanding. Encourage open dialogue to address broader family issues, ensuring everyone feels heard. This not only resolves the immediate conflict but also strengthens the family's emotional resilience. By consistently practicing these strategies, families can navigate challenges with grace and cohesion.

Consider the story of the Jones family, who consciously integrated emotional intelligence into their daily interactions. The parents prioritized emotional discussions at dinner, encouraging each child to share their feelings. Over time, the children developed a robust emotional vocabulary and empathy for one another. When disagreements arose, they were more equipped to handle them constructively, often resolving issues independently. This commitment to emotional growth transformed their family dynamics, creating a harmonious and supportive home environment.

11.2 A Sequential Roadmap to Emotional Growth

Imagine sitting at the end of a long day, reflecting not just on what you accomplished, but how you felt and interacted with others. Did you navigate stress with grace, or did it overwhelm you? Did you make judgments about colleagues, or did you remain curious about their perspectives? These moments of introspection are the foundation of emotional intelligence (EI) for personal growth.

EI is about creating space to observe, learn, and evolve. This chapter provides a roadmap to help you understand where you are now, envision where you want to go and develop the tools to get there. By the end, you'll recognize the power of EI and feel equipped to apply it to your unique goals, whether in the workplace or in your relationships.

Growth requires clarity, and clarity begins with reflection. To harness EI, follow this roadmap to guide your journey:

1. **Pause and Observe**
   - Start with awareness. Take note of your emotional responses during the day—both the positive and challenging moments. Did a colleague's comment trigger frustration? Did you feel energized during a brainstorming session?
   - **Reflection Questions:**
     - What emotions stood out to me today, and why?
     - Were there moments when I reacted instead of responding thoughtfully?

2. **Identify Patterns**
   - Over time, patterns emerge in how you respond to stress, criticism, or praise. Recognizing these helps you understand the root of your emotional reactions.
   - **Reflection Questions:**
     - Are there recurring triggers that consistently evoke similar emotions?
     - How do I typically respond to positive feedback or constructive criticism?

3. **Reframe Judgments as Observations**
   - Judgment limits growth. Observing without labeling allows you to see situations more objectively. For instance, instead of thinking, "They're so dismissive," consider, "They seem preoccupied; I wonder what's going on."
   - **Reflection Questions:**
     - What judgments did I make today?
     - How might I reframe these judgments into neutral observations?

4. **Track Progress**
   - Use a simple tool—a journal, spreadsheet, or phone app—to track your emotional responses and reflections. Documenting your growth reinforces awareness and helps you notice subtle changes over time.
   - **Reflection Questions:**
     - Where have I improved in managing my emotions?
     - What areas still feel challenging, and why?
5. **Set Emotional Goals**
   - Growth thrives on intention. Set goals that align with the emotional skills you want to develop, such as staying calm during disagreements or expressing gratitude more often.
   - **Reflection Questions:**
     - What specific emotional habits do I want to cultivate?
     - How will these changes improve my personal and professional relationships?

If you find the path a bit overwhelming at first, just stay with the first step: Pause and Observe. Get into the habit of learning to pause and observe by answering the two questions above. What emotions stood out to you, and were there moments when you reacted? Build the muscle of awareness with this step, answering the questions consistently each day. When it becomes a new habit and you feel more comfortable, continue down the roadmap.

11.3 Frameworks for Deepening Emotional Growth

To make the roadmap actionable, consider these frameworks:

1. **The CARE Framework for Emotional Reflection**
   - **C – Center Yourself:** Before reflecting, find a quiet space to pause and breathe.
   - **A – Acknowledge Emotions:** Name the emotions you experienced.

- R – **Revisit Key Moments:** Identify what triggered these emotions and how you reacted.
- E – **Explore Alternatives:** Consider how you might respond differently in the future.

2. **The SHIFT Model for Reframing Judgments**
   - S – **Stop:** Pause before reacting to a situation.
   - H – **Hear:** Listen to your internal dialogue.
   - I – **Identify Judgments:** Note any assumptions or labels.
   - F – **Frame Observations:** Turn judgments into neutral statements.
   - T – **Take Action:** Choose a constructive response based on observation.

3. **The GROW Framework for Goal-Setting**
   - G – **Goal:** Define the emotional skill you want to improve.
   - R – **Reality:** Assess where you are now.
   - O – **Options:** Brainstorm steps you can take to grow.
   - W – **Way Forward:** Commit to specific actions and timelines.

11.4 Personal and Professional Integration

EI influences more than your personal growth, breathing life into your relationships and workday as well.

- **In Relationships:** Use EI to navigate misunderstandings, resolve conflicts, and deepen emotional connections.
- **Reflection Questions:**
  - How often do I truly listen without planning my response?
  - When do I find it hardest to express empathy, and why?
- **In the Workplace:** EI enhances collaboration, resilience, and leadership. Apply it during meetings, feedback sessions, and team projects.
- **Reflection Questions:**
  - How do my emotions influence the tone of my interactions at work?

○ What steps can I take to foster trust and openness with my team?

11.5 A Reflection-Focused Conclusion

Your emotional growth journey isn't about fixing who you are—it's about discovering the best version of yourself. With each reflection, reframe, and goal you set, you take another step toward that vision.

Ask yourself:

- What does emotional growth mean to me?
- How will I know when I've made progress?
- What relationships or situations in my life can serve as "practice fields" for emotional intelligence?

With this roadmap, you have the tools to make choices that align with your values and aspirations. Growth is yours to own—step into it.

12. Practical Application and Future Directions

Picture yourself arriving at the office early in the morning, the quiet hum of the city awakening around you. As the elevator doors close, you take a moment to reflect on your emotional goals for the day. This practice is a strategic exercise in emotional intelligence. By setting intentions first thing in the morning, you align your emotional compass with your day's tasks, ensuring a balanced approach to the challenges ahead. This reflection helps ground you, providing clarity and purpose as you navigate the complexities of your work environment.

Integrating emotional intelligence into daily routines involves more than just morning reflections. Throughout the day, regular check-ins can be instrumental in maintaining emotional balance. Consider a brief midday pause, a moment to assess your emotional state. Are you feeling overwhelmed? Excited? Frustrated? This simple act of self-awareness allows you to recalibrate, addressing any emotional hurdles before they escalate. It acts as a reset button, helping you remain composed and focused, even amidst the chaos of back-to-back meetings or looming deadlines. By acknowledging your emotions, you empower yourself to manage them effectively, enhancing your productivity and well-being.

As evening falls and the day winds down, gratitude journaling offers another opportunity to cultivate emotional intelligence. Reflecting on positive experiences and expressing gratitude can shift your focus from stressors to achievements, fostering a sense of contentment and fulfillment. This practice promotes emotional well-being and enhances your relationships by encouraging empathy and understanding. By consistently acknowledging the positives, you cultivate an optimistic mindset, laying the foundation for resilience in the face of future challenges.

What will applying emotional intelligence to your personal interactions do for you and your relationships? In conversations with friends and family, empathy becomes a vital tool. By actively listening and seeking to understand their perspectives, you are able to build deeper connections, rooted in trust and mutual respect. This skill is equally beneficial in professional settings, where empathy can bridge gaps and resolve conflicts. Practicing active listening during daily interactions demonstrates genuine interest and concern, reinforcing bonds and improving communication.

Using emotional intelligence for personal decision-making can also be transformative. When faced with significant choices, creating emotional pros and cons lists can provide valuable insights. How do you feel about each pro and con? By considering the emotional impact of each option, you can make informed decisions that align with your values and goals. Reflective questioning further enhances this process, helping you uncover the emotional drivers behind your choices. This introspection fosters self-awareness, enabling you to make decisions confidently.

12.1 Interactive Element: Emotional Intelligence Integration Checklist

To deepen your practice and create actionable insights, here's an expanded checklist with guided questions for each phase of your day. These prompts will help you engage more meaningfully with your emotional journey and make choices that align with your goals and values.

Morning Reflection: Setting Emotional Intentions

Begin your day with a clear emotional focus. Think about the tone you want to set and the relationships you want to nurture.

- **Questions to Reflect On:**
    1. What emotional state do I want to embody today (e.g., calm, focused, empathetic)?
    2. What challenges might arise, and how can I prepare emotionally for them?
    3. Which relationships or tasks require my full presence today?
    4. How can I prioritize connection and understanding in my interactions?
    5. If stress arises, what tools (e.g., deep breathing, pausing) will I use to stay grounded
- **Suggested Action:** Write a one-sentence emotional intention for the day. For example: "Today, I approach every interaction with patience and curiosity."

Midday Check-In: Assessing and Recalibrating

Take a moment during your day to pause, evaluate your emotions, and make adjustments.

- **Questions to Reflect On:**
  1. What emotions have surfaced so far today, and what triggered them?
  2. Are there any stressors affecting my focus or mood?
  3. Have I maintained my morning emotional intention, or have I drifted? Why?
  4. What judgmental thoughts have I noticed about myself or others? How can I reframe them?
  5. What's one small action I can take right now to reset or realign (e.g., a quick stretch, a brief walk, or a mindful breath)?
- **Suggested Action:** Set a mini-goal for the afternoon, such as improving a conversation, tackling a challenging task with focus, or offering support to someone in need.

Evening Reflection: Gratitude and Growth

End your day with gratitude and insights to carry forward.

- **Questions to Reflect On:**
  1. What went well today, and how did those moments impact my emotions?
  2. What challenges did I face, and how did I handle them emotionally?
  3. Where did I succeed in staying aligned with my emotional intentions?
  4. What judgments did I make today, and how might I approach those situations differently tomorrow?
  5. Who or what am I most grateful for today, and why?

Suggested Action: Write down three things you're grateful for and reflect on how they shaped your emotional state. Then, consider one emotional habit or insight to work on tomorrow.

Weekly Reflection: Tracking Emotional Patterns

At the end of the week, step back to observe trends and growth.

- **Questions to Reflect On:**
  1. What recurring emotions did I notice this week, and what were the triggers?
  2. How did I handle stress or conflict over the past few days?
  3. Which emotional goals did I meet, and where can I improve?
  4. What relationships felt strengthened, and what contributed to that?
  5. What judgmental patterns emerged, and how can I reframe them moving forward?
- **Suggested Action:** Use your insights to set one emotional goal for the week ahead. Write it down and identify a small step you'll take each day to work toward it.

Stories of individuals successfully integrating emotional intelligence into their daily lives provide inspiration and practical insights. Consider a parent who uses EI to navigate the challenges of raising children. By practicing empathy and emotional regulation, they cultivate a supportive environment that encourages open communication and emotional growth. In the workplace, professionals who apply EI in collaboration and problem-solving often discover increased team cohesion and productivity. Their ability to manage emotions and understand colleagues' perspectives leads to more effective teamwork and innovative solutions.

12.2 Developing Customizable Self-Assessment Tools

In fast-paced corporate environments, decisions are made in the blink of an eye. To stay ahead, mastering one's emotional landscape becomes a game-changer. This is where self-assessment tools come into play, acting as mirrors that reflect our emotional strengths and weaknesses. They provide personalized insights, crucial for anyone aiming to enhance their emotional intelligence. By identifying these areas, you can set targeted goals, allowing for focused development in your EI journey. These tools serve as a foundation, helping you map out a path for growth that aligns with your personal and professional aspirations.

Creating tailored self-assessment tools is an exercise in introspection and customization. Begin by designing questions that directly address your unique challenges and experiences. This personalization ensures that the insights you gather are relevant and actionable. For instance, if managing stress in high-pressure meetings is a concern, include questions that explore your emotional responses in such scenarios. Incorporating feedback from trusted peers can enrich this process. Their perspectives offer an external view of your emotional interactions, shedding light on areas you might overlook. This collaborative approach enhances the accuracy of your assessment and fosters a deeper understanding of your emotional dynamics.

Regular implementation of self-assessment practices is key to maintaining momentum in your emotional development. Set aside time each month for self-reflection sessions, allowing you to track your progress and adjust your goals as needed. These sessions provide a moment of pause in the demanding corporate environment, helping you recalibrate and refocus. Periodic peer feedback and review further augment this practice. Encouraging colleagues to share their observations creates an environment of mutual growth and support. In today's digital age, utilizing technology for continuous tracking can be invaluable. Digital tools offer convenience and precision, enabling you to monitor emotional trends and patterns over time.

The effectiveness of self-assessment tools is evident in various professional settings. Educators, for example, have adapted these tools to stimulate student growth, encouraging young minds to explore their emotional worlds. By integrating self-assessment into their curriculum, they equip students with the skills needed to navigate complex social landscapes. In corporate spheres, leaders have leveraged 360-degree feedback to enhance team dynamics. This comprehensive approach provides a holistic view of an individual's emotional impact, guiding improvements in leadership and collaboration. These examples underscore the transformative potential of self-assessment tools, illustrating how they can drive meaningful change in both personal and professional contexts.

Consider the case of a senior manager at a tech firm who utilized self-assessment to refine her leadership style. By regularly evaluating her emotional responses to team interactions, she identified a tendency to become defensive during feedback sessions. With this insight, she focused on developing her emotional regulation skills, leading to more constructive dialogues and a more cohesive team environment. Her journey highlights the power of tailored self-assessment tools in facilitating personal growth and enhancing workplace relationships. Similarly, an educator implementing self-assessment in the classroom noted increased emotional awareness among students. As a result of her efforts, she created a more empathetic and supportive learning environment.

12.3 Investing in Emotional Education and Development

As the world accelerates, emotional education is more important than ever. It is a key component of both personal and professional development. Emotional intelligence training in schools and workplaces yields numerous benefits. It fosters empathy, allowing individuals to connect more deeply with others. Moreover, it builds resilience, equipping people to handle life's challenges with grace and composure. These skills are invaluable, as they not only enhance individual well-being but also contribute to a more harmonious and productive environment, whether in the classroom or boardroom.

Current trends in emotional education reveal a growing recognition of its importance across various sectors. Educational institutions are increasingly integrating emotional intelligence curricula, teaching students to recognize and manage their emotions from an early age. This early intervention lays the foundation for lifelong emotional health. In the corporate world, initiatives are promoting emotional development through workshops and training programs. These initiatives aim to create emotionally intelligent workforces capable of navigating complex interpersonal dynamics within a more positve organizational culture. Companies are beginning to see that investing in emotional education is not just a perk but a necessity for sustainable success.

For individuals and organizations looking to invest in emotional education, several strategies can be effective. Start by identifying suitable training programs and workshops that align with specific needs and goals. Encouraging lifelong learning in emotional intelligence should be a priority, as it ensures continuous growth and adaptation. Partnering with experts can provide tailored emotional education that addresses unique challenges and opportunities. By taking these steps, you equip yourself and your organization with the tools needed to thrive in an emotionally intelligent manner.

Successful emotional education initiatives abound, offering valuable lessons and inspiration. Schools that have implemented emotional intelligence programs often report significant improvements in student well-being and academic performance. These programs teach students to manage stress, communicate effectively, and resolve conflicts peacefully. In the workplace, organizations that prioritize emotional education benefit from enhanced culture and increased employee engagement. Employees become more collaborative, innovative, and satisfied, leading to improved overall performance. These examples demonstrate the transformative power of emotional education, making it clear that investing in emotional development is a wise and impactful endeavor.

12.4 Future Trends in Emotional Intelligence Research

In recent years, emotional intelligence has expanded beyond traditional human interactions, finding its place within the realm of technology. One of the most intriguing areas of research is the integration of emotional intelligence into artificial intelligence and machine learning systems. As AI evolves, developers are striving to create machines that can not only perform tasks but also understand and respond to human emotions. This involves programming AI to recognize subtle emotional cues, such as tone of voice or facial expressions, and respond in ways that are empathetic and appropriate. This fusion of technology and emotional intelligence could revolutionize fields like customer service and healthcare, where understanding human emotions enhances user experience and outcomes.

Cross-cultural studies have also become a focal point in emotional intelligence research. These studies delve into how emotional expression and understanding vary across different cultures. For instance, a gesture that is considered a sign of respect in one culture might be perceived differently in another. Researchers are exploring these nuances to develop a more inclusive understanding of emotional intelligence that transcends cultural boundaries. This research not only enriches our comprehension of global emotional dynamics but also informs how we implement EI training in diverse environments, ensuring it is both effective and culturally sensitive.

Technological advancements have brought about significant changes in how we develop and apply emotional intelligence. Virtual reality, for instance, is being leveraged as an innovative tool for empathy training. By immersing individuals in virtual environments that simulate real-world emotional scenarios, VR allows them to experience and respond to emotions in a controlled setting. This experiential learning approach can deepen empathy and improve emotional responses in real-life situations. Additionally, AI-driven emotional analysis tools are gaining traction. These tools assess emotional data from various sources, providing insights into emotional trends and patterns that can inform personal and organizational development.

Innovative research studies and initiatives continue to shape the future of emotional intelligence. Universities are at the forefront of this exploration, establishing dedicated programs focused on EI research. These programs bring together interdisciplinary teams to study various aspects of emotional intelligence, from its neurological basis to its practical applications. Corporate partnerships are also playing a crucial role, with companies collaborating with academic institutions to explore how EI can be applied in business settings. These collaborations aim to enhance leadership capabilities, improve team dynamics, and drive organizational success through the strategic application of emotional intelligence principles.

As research and technology advance, the landscape of emotional intelligence continues to evolve. From artificial intelligence to cross-cultural studies, the possibilities are vast and varied. These developments promise to deepen our understanding of emotional intelligence while simultaneously expanding its applications in both personal and professional contexts. Whether through immersive virtual reality experiences or innovative educational programs, the future holds exciting potential for those willing to embrace the evolving nature of emotional intelligence

12.5 Cultivating a Legacy of Emotional Intelligence

Imagine a world where everyday life is imbued with emotional intelligence (EI), passed down from one generation to the next, much like cherished family traditions. This vision begins with us, the current torchbearers of EI, as we play a pivotal role in nurturing these skills in future generations. The importance of instilling emotional intelligence in our youth cannot be overstated. Through mentoring programs, we can guide young minds to understand and regulate their emotions, nurturing empathy and resilience from an early age. These programs can take various forms, from school-based initiatives to community-led efforts, each designed to equip children with the emotional tools needed to thrive in a complex world. Additionally, within our own families, we can create environments that promote emotional growth. Simple activities like family discussions about emotions or collaborative problem-solving exercises can teach children valuable lessons in empathy and emotional regulation.

Communities and organizations also have a vital role in promoting emotional intelligence. By fostering a culture that values and teaches EI, we can create environments where emotional skills are recognized as essential to success and well-being. Community workshops focused on EI awareness can bring people together, providing a space to learn and share experiences. These gatherings encourage individuals to explore their emotional landscapes and develop the skills necessary for personal and collective growth. Organizations, too, can prioritize EI by integrating it into their training programs and corporate values. This commitment not only enhances employee satisfaction and productivity but also cultivates a workplace culture that values emotional understanding.

Advocating for emotional intelligence is a continuous journey, one that requires dedication and passion. As we become advocates for EI, we inspire others to embrace these skills and recognize their transformative power. Hosting seminars and discussions on emotional intelligence can spark interest and dialogue, encouraging others to explore their own emotional capacities. Sharing our personal journeys with EI, whether through writing or public speaking, offers valuable insights and motivates others to embark on their own paths of emotional discovery. By championing EI, we create ripples of change that extend beyond our immediate circles, impacting communities and organizations in profound ways.

As we cultivate a legacy of emotional intelligence, we lay the groundwork for a future where empathy, understanding, and emotional resilience are not just valued but celebrated. This work requires ongoing commitment and collaboration, but the rewards are immeasurable. By fostering EI in future generations and promoting it within our communities and organizations, we contribute to a world where emotional intelligence is a cornerstone of personal and collective success. Through our actions, we ensure that this legacy endures, shaping a future where emotional intelligence is accessible to all.

12.6 Conclusion

As you close this book, I hope you feel empowered and inspired to embrace the transformational journey of emotional intelligence. Throughout our exploration, we've demystified emotional intelligence, revealing it as a dynamic skill that anyone can develop. No longer just an inherent trait, emotional intelligence is a learnable and vital ability, encompassing self-awareness, self-management, social awareness, and relationship management.

The importance of emotional intelligence in both personal and professional realms cannot be overstated. By mastering these skills, you enhance your leadership capabilities, manage stress effectively, communicate with clarity, and build richer, more meaningful relationships. These abilities are integral to your career success, and they are also key to a balanced and fulfilling personal life.

Our shared vision has been to guide you on the path to becoming an emotionally intelligent leader, someone who can navigate the complexities of modern life with grace and understanding. By investing in emotional education and development, you open doors to personal growth and professional advancement. These investments, while offering personal gain, also hold the potential to uplift the teams and communities around you.

I encourage you to champion emotional education, not only for yourself but within your organization and community. Advocate for workshops, courses, and programs that nurture emotional growth. By doing so, you contribute to a culture where emotional skills are valued and developed, creating a ripple effect that can transform environments and improve collective well-being.

As you move forward, I urge you to integrate the strategies and exercises from this book into your daily life. Emotional intelligence is not a one-time achievement but a lifelong pursuit. Regular practice and reflection will deepen your understanding and enhance your skills. Make it a habit to assess your emotional responses, engage in active listening, and practice empathy every day.

Engagement with others on this journey can be incredibly rewarding. Share your experiences and insights with those around you. Form or join discussion groups, workshops, or online forums dedicated to emotional intelligence. These interactions offer dual benefits: they reinforce your learning while building a community of like-minded individuals committed to personal and collective growth.

Your journey doesn't end here. Think of the legacy you can create by passing on the knowledge and skills you've acquired. Teach future generations the value of emotional intelligence, ensuring that these vital skills are embedded into their daily lives. By doing so, you contribute to a lasting culture of empathy, understanding, and emotional resilience.

Thank you for allowing me to accompany you on this journey. Your dedication to personal development and leadership is commendable. I am grateful for your trust and commitment, and I am excited about the positive impact you will make in your life and the lives of others.

Remember, emotional intelligence is a powerful tool for achieving personal fulfillment and professional excellence. As you continue to develop these skills, you will find yourself more connected, more empathetic, and more capable of leading with integrity and heart. Embrace this journey with enthusiasm, and watch as it transforms your world.

References

EI Overview: The Four Domains and Twelve Competencies https://danielgolemanemotional intelligence.com/ei-overview-the-four-domains-and-twelve-competencies/

Emotional intelligence is associated with connectivity ... https://pmc.ncbi.nlm.nih.gov/arti cles/PMC5737574/

The Business Case for Emotional Intelligence https://rw360.org/wp-content/uploads/ 2024/02/Business-Case-for-EI.pdf

Empathy In Leadership: Importance, Benefits, & Examples https://managementconsulted. com/empathy-in-leadership/

Debunking 10 Common Emotional Intelligence Myths https://www.linkedin.com/pulse/ debunking-10-common-emotional-intelligence-myths-john-rampton-1e

Emotional Intelligence Improves Leadership at FedEx https://www.6seconds.org/2014/01/ 14/case-study-emotional-intelligence-people-first-leadership-fedex-express/

The Invisible Wall of Psychological Resistance https://whywesuffer.com/the-invisible-wall-of-psychological-resistance/

How to Use Emotional Intelligence to Handle Career Setbacks https://www.linkedin.com/ advice/3/how-can-you-use-emotional-intelligence-handle-f26sc#:

How To Deal With Emotional Triggers At Work: 4 Effective ... https://brainleadership.com/ how-to-deal-with-emotional-triggers-at-work/

Mastering Non-Judgmental Observation https://liveinspiredcounselling.com/blogs/f/ mastering-non-judgmental-observation

17 Emotional Intelligence Tests & Assessments (+ Free Quiz) https://positivepsychology. com/emotional-intelligence-tests/

Mindfulness and Emotion Regulation https://pmc.ncbi.nlm.nih.gov/articles/ PMC5337506/

Improving Emotional Intelligence (EQ): Expert Guide https://www.helpguide.org/mental-health/wellbeing/emotional-intelligence-eq

The power of language: How words shape thoughts and ... https://www.bonn-institute.org/ en/news/psychology-in-journalism-2

4 Ways Mindfulness Traits and Practices Build Resilience https://www.psychologytoday. com/us/blog/mindfulness-insights/202103/4-ways-mindfulness-traits-and-prac tices-build-resilience

Ability of Emotional Regulation and Control as a Stress ... https://www.ncbi.nlm.nih.gov/ pmc/articles/PMC9819563/

The Importance Of Empathy In Leadership: How To Lead ... https://www.forbes.com/sites/ karadennison/2023/02/24/the-importance-of-empathy-in-leadership-how-to-lead-with-compassion-and-understanding-in-2023/

Beyond Words: The Power of Body Language in Intercultural ... https://tanjafromnuminos.

medium.com/beyond-words-the-power-of-body-language-in-intercultural-commu nication-62cfc2df410e

Active Listening: Definition, Skills, & Benefits https://www.simplypsychology.org/active-listening-definition-skills-benefits.html

How Emotional Intelligence Can Enhance Cross-Cultural ... https://ei4change.com/how-emotional-intelligence-can-enhance-cross-cultural-communication/

20 Trust-Building Exercises and Activities for Teams https://www.snowhr.com/BlogDetail/ 224/20-trust-building-exercises-and-activities-for-teams/0/all-categories

How Emotional Intelligence Became a Key Leadership Skill https://hbr.org/2015/04/how-emotional-intelligence-became-a-key-leadership-skill

10 Examples of Constructive Feedback in the Workplace https://www.indeed.com/career-advice/career-development/constructive-feedback-examples

Manage a Difficult Conversation with Emotional Intelligence https://hbr.org/2014/06/ manage-a-difficult-conversation-with-emotional-intelligence

Emotional Intelligence and Leadership Effectiveness - Ccl.org https://www.ccl.org/articles/ leading-effectively-articles/emotional-intelligence-and-leadership-effectiveness/

Building the Emotional Intelligence of Groups https://hbr.org/2001/03/building-the-emotional-intelligence-of-groups

Emotional Agility https://hbr.org/2013/11/emotional-agility

Navigating Office Politics: 5 Strategies For A Successful Career https://spearhead.so/navigat ing-office-politics-5-strategies-for-a-successful-career/

A Business Case For Emotional Intelligence For Leaders https://www.forbes.com/councils/ forbescoachescouncil/2023/10/02/a-business-case-for-emotional-intelligence-for-leaders/

The Importance Of Emotional Intelligence At Work https://www.forbes.com/councils/ forbeshumanresourcescouncil/2023/07/18/the-importance-of-emotional-intelli gence-at-work/

The Secret Weapon of Great Leaders: Emotional Intelligence https://www.linkedin.com/ pulse/secret-weapon-great-leaders-emotional-intelligence-edge-ikope

How to Develop Emotional Intelligence Skills - HBS Online https://online.hbs.edu/blog/ post/emotional-intelligence-skills

Stress appraisal in the workplace and its associations with ... https://pmc.ncbi.nlm.nih.gov/ articles/PMC10760677/#:

Job burnout: How to spot it and take action https://www.mayoclinic.org/healthy-lifestyle/ adult-health/in-depth/burnout/art-20046642

Meditation and Mindfulness: Effectiveness and Safety | NCCIH https://www.nccih.nih.gov/ health/meditation-and-mindfulness-effectiveness-and-safety

Adapting to Change Requires Flexible Leaders - Ccl.org https://www.ccl.org/articles/lead ing-effectively-articles/adaptability-1-idea-3-facts-5-tips/#:

The Role of Emotional Intelligence in Conflict Resolution https://cpdonline.co.uk/knowl edge-base/mental-health/emotional-intelligence-conflict-resolution/

Why Empathy Is Necessary in Negotiation https://www.shapironegotiations.com/blog/ why-empathy-is-necessary-in-negotiation/

Case Study of Conflict Management: To Resolve Disputes ... https://www.pon.harvard.edu/daily/conflict-resolution/telling-the-third-story/

Using Emotional Intelligence And Respect To Resolve ... https://www.forbes.com/councils/forbescoachescouncil/2024/07/31/using-emotional-intelligence-and-respect-to-resolve-conflict-in-the-workplace-an-executive-coachs-perspective/

The Importance of Emotional Intelligence in Personal Growth https://www.coachingly.ai/blog/single/the-importance-of-emotional-intelligence-in-personal-growth

Developing Emotional Intelligence through Reflective ... https://everydayspeech.com/sel-implementation/developing-emotional-intelligence-through-reflective-thinking-the-think-it-dont-say-it-method/

Emotional Intelligence: The Key to Lasting Relationships https://fatherhoodchannel.com/2024/10/08/emotional-intelligence-the-key-to-lasting-relationships/

4 of the best tools to measure and assess Emotional ... https://www.rochemartin.com/blog/best-tools-emotional-intelligence

13 Emotional Intelligence Activities, Exercises & PDFs https://positivepsychology.com/emotional-intelligence-exercises/

4 of the best tools to measure and assess Emotional ... https://www.rochemartin.com/blog/best-tools-emotional-intelligence

Editorial: New trends in emotional intelligence https://www.frontiersin.org/journals/psychology/articles/10.3389/fpsyg.2023.1266076/full

Youth Emotional Intelligence: Why Teaching them Young Can ... https://www.youtheducationdevelopment.com/post/youth-emotional-intelligence-why-teaching-them-young-can-lead-to-their-success

Fiske, S. T., Cuddy, A. J. C., & Glick, P. (2007). *The stereotype content model: Understanding social perception through warmth and competence. Trends in Cognitive Sciences, 11(2),* 77–83.

Harris, L. T., & Fiske, S. T. (2006). *Dehumanizing the lowest of the low: Neuroimaging responses to extreme outgroups. Psychological Science, 17(10),* 847–853.

Goleman, D. (1995). *Emotional intelligence: Why it can matter more than IQ.* Bantam Books.

Heffernan, M. (2012). *Wilful blindness: Why we ignore the obvious at our peril.* Simon & Schuster.

Brown, B. (2018). *Dare to lead: Brave work. Tough conversations. Whole hearts.* Random House.

Appendix A: A Step-by-Step Guide to Reframing Judgments into Observations

1. **Pause and Acknowledge the Judgment**
   - Recognize the thought for what it is: a judgment, not a fact. Acknowledge it without self-criticism.
   - Example: "I just judged my coworker as lazy for missing a deadline."
2. **Separate Facts from Assumptions**
   - Ask yourself: What do I know for certain, and what am I assuming?
     - Fact: "The deadline was missed."
     - Assumption: "They didn't care enough to complete the task."
3. **Reframe with Neutral Language**
   - Turn the judgment into a neutral observation by describing what happened without attaching a value.
     - Observation: "The deadline was missed, and I'm unsure why."
4. **Consider Alternative Explanations**
   - Practice empathy by imagining other reasons for the situation.
     - Thought: "Maybe they were overwhelmed or misunderstood the timeline."

5. **Take a Constructive Next Step**
    - Use your observation to decide on a constructive action, such as asking questions for clarification or offering support.
        - Action: "I'll check in to understand what happened and how we can avoid this in the future."

Appendix B: Compass of Clear Communication
(based on the work of Jim Bunch and Coach Sean Smith)

In order to gain commitment to change behaviors, it requires that we not judge but state the observation and how that observation impacted you personally. When done correctly, you maintain the other person's dignity while authentically sharing how the impact of their behavior affected you. In the end, you can gain commitment to the new behavior going forward.

This communication can be used with subordinates, co-workers, managers, spouses, children...anyone to truly share your vulnerability while extending a strong and clear invitation to redirect the behavior.

In every situation when you observe something that is not desirable that may need redirecting, use this sentence structure below:

Sentence Stem

When _____ (*state the observation*) happened, I made it mean _____ (*your judgment of the observation*). Because of that, I felt _____ (*state the emotion that your judgment created in you in that moment*).

What I really want to feel is that _____ (*state your desired emotion*). So my request is _____ (*redirect the behavior*). Are you willing to fulfill that?

Subordinate Example

When you left early without asking me *(observation)*, I made it mean that you do not respect my authority *(your judgment of the observation)*. Because of that, I felt very angry and disappointed in you *(the emotion your judgment created in you as a result)*. What I really want to feel is that I can trust you *(state your desired emotion)*. So my request is going forward, ask me first before leaving *(state your desired emotion)*. Are you willing to fulfill that?

- When you speak this way, you will find out why the person really left early. Perhaps there was an emergency and they judged that it would be ok to leave without asking since it was an emergency.
- Meanwhile, you judged them as insensitive and not caring about respecting you as a leader.
- This sentence stem will do the following:
  - Clear up their intention
  - Allow you to understand their logic
  - Redirect their behavior respectfully. Almost everyone will agree yes.
- In the event, you have some that say NO to fulfilling your request, then be willing to take the next steps. With a subordinate, then share with them that in the future, should they do it again, you will advance them to a verbal warning so that they understand their boundaries.

Spousal Example

When didn't come home at your usual time *(observation)*, I made it mean that you didn't think it is important to let me know your where-abouts *(your judgment of the observation)*. Because of that, I felt very upset and wondered what you were doing *(the emotion your judgment created in you as a result)*.

What I really want to feel is that <u>if you are late, you will let me know what's going so that I feel that you care</u> (*state your desired emotion*). So my request is <u>going forward, please call me if you are going to be late</u> (*state your desired emotion*). Are you willing to fulfill that?

- Rather than implying your spouse should automatically know how you feel in your head, speaking directly when certain observations that you notice are not ok with you make it more clear to the other person what you think and how you feel.
- Now they have a chance to understand you and make the adjustment.
- Again, most spouses will probably say yes if they didn't realize how their actions were impacting you. Maybe they grew up independently and are still grappling with how to go from an "I" to a "we" after you both say "I do" at the marriage ceremony. This typeof clear language gives a chance to see their intentions and their heart.
- Now, if your spouse says NO, then you may have other things to consider. But at least it is clear.

Appendix C: A Practical Guide on How to Conduct Regular Check-ins

Regular check-ins serve as critical milestones on the journey of emotional development, offering a structured framework for monitoring advancements, engaging in sincere self-reflection, and fine-tuning your emotional strategies accordingly. Embracing these structured check-ins illuminates the intricate patterns of your emotional behaviors, providing a clear path to addressing them and fostering sustained emotional intelligence growth. To optimize the benefits derived from these reflective sessions, adhere to the following detailed guide:

1. **Schedule Consistent Times for Reflection**
    - Choose specific times in your day or week to pause and evaluate your emotional state. Consistency helps establish this practice as a natural part of your daily life.
        - **Daily:** Spend 5–10 minutes in the morning, midday, and evening.
        - **Weekly:** Dedicate 15–30 minutes at the end of the week for a more in-depth review, allowing for broader insights and adjustments.
2. **Create a Safe Space for Reflection**
    - Find a quiet, distraction-free environment where you can focus on your inner self without interruptions. This might be a corner of your home, a quiet park, or even your car before starting work.

3. **Ask Specific, Guiding Questions**
   - The key to effective check-ins is asking meaningful questions that encourage honest reflection. Consider these prompts:
     - **Morning Check-In:**
       - What emotional state do I want to cultivate today?
       - What is one small action I can take to stay grounded and focused?
     - **Midday Check-In:**
       - How am I feeling right now, and what triggered this emotion?
       - Have I acted in alignment with my emotional goals for the day?
       - What adjustments can I make to improve the rest of my day?
     - **Evening Check-In:**
       - What were the highlights of my day, and how did they make me feel?
       - What challenges did I face, and how did I handle them emotionally?
       - What would I like to carry forward into tomorrow?
4. **Use Tracking Tools to Log Insights**
   - Write down your reflections to track progress over time. Use tools that work best for you:
     - **Journals:** Write entries by hand or digitally to capture your thoughts and patterns.
     - **Spreadsheets:** Create columns for the date, emotions, triggers, actions, and lessons learned.
     - **Phone Notes:** Keep quick, on-the-go observations in your phone's notes app.

5. **Celebrate Small Wins and Identify Patterns**
   - **Celebrate Wins:** Note moments when you handled a situation with greater emotional awareness or effectively managed stress. Recognizing progress boosts motivation.
   - **Identify Patterns:** Look for recurring triggers, emotional responses, or behaviors. These patterns provide valuable insights into areas for growth.
6. **Be Honest and Gentle with Yourself**
   - Regular check-ins are not meant for self-criticism—they're opportunities for awareness and growth. When reflecting on areas for improvement, frame them constructively:
     - Instead of: "I'm terrible at staying calm during meetings."
     - Try: "I noticed that I struggled to stay calm today. Next time, I'll try taking a few deep breaths before responding."
7. **Revisit and Adjust Your Goals**
   - Use insights from your check-ins to refine your emotional goals. As you grow, you might set more specific intentions or explore new areas of emotional intelligence to develop.

Appendix D: Empowering Language Versus Disempowering Language

The words we use, both out loud and in our thoughts, profoundly shape how we feel and behave. Words have an energy associated with them. Negative words tend to make us feel lower, while positive words tend to make us feel higher and better. Pay close attention to the words or phrasing you use. Consider replacing some of the more common disempowering words that we use that tend to remove a person's choice with empowering words that embed choice. Notice how others begin to respond to these small tweaks that you make!

DISEMPOWERING EMPOWERING

I *have to* do that. I **get the opportunity** to do that.

I *need to* do that. I **have the chance** to do that.

I *should* do that. I'll **consider** doing that.

I *always* do that. I do that **on occasion**.

I *never* do that. I **don't** do that *often*.

Why is this happening? **How** can I overcome this?

Appendix E: Navigating Perceived Politics

If you are unsure whether office politics are happening or not, notice if you are judging or observing. This shift will help you find center and regain control of the only person you have control over: you:

Framework: The ASK Model for Perceived Politics

To navigate perceived politics while avoiding the pitfalls of judgment, use the **ASK** model:

- **A – Acknowledge Your Feelings**
  - Recognize how the uncertainty makes you feel—whether it's suspicion, anxiety, or frustration. Validating your emotions allows you to manage them instead of being controlled by them.
- **S – Seek Facts, Not Assumptions**
  - Pause and ask: *What do I actually know for sure?* Separate what's observable (e.g., meetings are happening) from what's assumed (e.g., they're plotting against me).
- **K – Keep Communication Open**
  - Engage in conversations that clarify rather than fuel assumptions. For example, you might say, *"I noticed there's been a lot of discussion about the project. Is there anything I can do to contribute?"* This opens a door for transparency and builds trust.

Appendix F: Navigating Active Politics When the Game is Real

In active politics, there is no doubt. The manager brags in front of you what he can do with his power. You see that credit is stolen and given to others, inappropriate relationships that favor those that "kiss the ring" of the supervisor and so much more.

To regain center to be able to reground and think strategically, follow the P.A.T.H. Framework:

Framework: The PATH Method for Active Politics

To handle active politics with clarity and emotional intelligence, follow the **PATH** method:

- **P – Pause and Reflect**
  - Before reacting, take a moment to process. What are you observing, and how does it make you feel? This step helps prevent reactive decisions and allows for thoughtful responses.
- **A – Analyze Motivations**
  - Consider what might be driving the political behavior. Is someone vying for recognition? Protecting their position? Understanding these dynamics helps you depersonalize the situation.
- **T – Take Strategic Actions**
  - Decide on your next steps based on observation, not judgment. This might include documenting your

contributions, building alliances with trusted colleagues, or seeking mentorship to navigate the landscape.

- **H – Hold Your Integrity**
  - Stay true to your values, even in a challenging environment. Engage in transparent, ethical communication, and resist the urge to stoop to political tactics that undermine trust.

Appendix G: The Roadmap to Deepening Emotional Growth

To make the emotional intelligence roadmap actionable, consider these frameworks:

1. **The CARE Framework for Emotional Reflection**
   - **C – Center Yourself:** Before reflecting, find a quiet space to pause and breathe.
   - **A – Acknowledge Emotions:** Name the emotions you experienced.
   - **R – Revisit Key Moments:** Identify what triggered these emotions and how you reacted.
   - **E – Explore Alternatives:** Consider how you might respond differently in the future.
2. **The SHIFT Model for Reframing Judgments**
   - **S – Stop:** Pause before reacting to a situation.
   - **H – Hear:** Listen to your internal dialogue.
   - **I – Identify Judgments:** Note any assumptions or labels.
   - **F – Frame Observations:** Turn judgments into neutral statements.
   - **T – Take Action:** Choose a constructive response based on observation.

3. **The GROW Framework for Goal-Setting**
   - **G – Goal:** Define the emotional skill you want to improve.
   - **R – Reality:** Assess where you are now.
   - **O – Options:** Brainstorm steps you can take to grow.
   - **W – Way Forward:** Commit to specific actions and timelines.

Made in the USA
Las Vegas, NV
15 February 2025

18210522R00095